BEYOND THE WORDS

BEYOND THE WORDS

ALSO BY BONNI GOLDBERG

NONFICTION

*Gifts from the Heart: Meditations on Caring
for Aging Parents (with Geo Kendall)*

Room to Write: Daily Invitations to a Writer's Life

ANTHOLOGY

The Spirit of Pregnancy

logy, Reflections On The Gift Of The Watermelon Pic

les and that title made it clear I was not the only one who

retly loved (no fifth grader in her right mind would admit)

tching poetry into my brain, when she announ an upcoming

ever occurred to me to write a poem myself. Nobody asked

for many years. I wrote three poems. They all rhymed. I

contest. I won. Not the contest; I never heard a word

writing in the fifth grade. It all began with poetry. Ex

logy, Reflections On The Gift Of The Watermelon Pic

les and that title made it clear I was not the only one who

retly loved (no fifth grader in her right ind would admit

tching poetry into my brain, when she announced an upcom

f had never occurred to me to write a poem myself. Nobody

lt for many years. I wrote three poems. They all rhymed.

the contest. I won. Not the contest; I never heard a wor

writing in the fifth grade. It all began with poetry. Ex

logy, Reflections On The Gift Of The Watermelon Pic

les and that title made it clear I was not the only one who

BEYOND THE WORDS

The Three Untapped Sources

of Creative Fulfillment

for Writers

BONNI GOLDBERG

JEREMY P. TARCHER/PUTNAM

a member of Penguin Group (USA) Inc.

New York

Most Tarcher/Putnam books are available at special quantity
discounts for bulk purchase for sales promotions, premiums,
fund-raising, and educational needs. Special books or book excerpts
also can be created to fit specific needs. For details, write Putnam
Special Markets, 375 Hudson Street, New York, NY 10014.

Jeremy P. Tarcher/Putnam
a member of
Penguin Group (USA) Inc.
375 Hudson Street
New York, NY 10014
www.penguin.com

First paperback edition 2003

The Library of Congress has catalogued the hardcover edition
as follows:

Goldberg, Bonni.
Beyond the words : the three untapped sources of creative
fulfillment for writers / Bonni Goldberg.
p.   cm.
ISBN 1-58542-155-3
1. Authorship.   I. Title.
PN147 .G59   2002   2001052733
808'.02—dc21

ISBN 1-58542-224-X (Paperback edition)

This book is printed on acid-free paper. ⊗

Printed in the United States of America
1   3   5   7   9   10   8   6   4   2

Book design by Jennifer Ann Daddio

*To those who show me how
to be grateful and respectful,
and to those who helped me
learn the meaning of enough
and to measure success
by the joy in my heart.*

Acknowledgments

I am indebted to

My publishing community: Jeremy Tarcher, Wendy Hubbert, and Joel Fotinos; and the dynamic duo, Lisa Swayne and Susan Berry.

My writing community, especially Joanna C. Scott, Natasha Sajé, Brandel France de Bravo, Lisa Cohn, Catherine Paglin, Elizabeth Rusch, Nichola Zaklan, and Robert Rumbolz.

My soul-soothing community, especially Alison Yahana, Devorah Spilman, and Rebbitzin Devora Wilhelm.

My dear family: Isabel, I'm sorry I was too busy this year. And Geo, thank you for waving me on no matter what, as you nurtured our daughter (fantastically) and tended to our home while I wrote.

CONTENTS

II. REVISION

⌒

III. GOING PUBLIC

Love the words
and beyond the words.

ANONYMOUS

INTRODUCTION

I started writing in the fifth grade. It all began with poetry. Every two weeks, my teacher, Mrs. Thaine, made us memorize a poem out of our anthology, *Reflections on a Gift of Watermelon Pickle*. It was the strangest title I'd ever heard, but I loved eating watermelon pickles and that title made it clear I was not the only one who appreciated them.

So because I felt an affinity with a title that praised something I secretly loved (no fifth-grader in her right mind would admit to eating such a thing, much less looking forward to it) and because Mrs. Thaine was etching poetry into my brain, when she announced a student contest from a notice she'd received, I wrote my first poems. Until then it had never occurred to me to write a poem myself. Nobody asked me to do it. I just decided to do it—a reason I would rarely allow myself as an adult for many years.

I wrote three poems. They all rhymed. I had no idea where they had come from, but I didn't ask questions. I sent them in to the contest.

I won. Not the contest; I never heard a word from the contest. But I won a voice and a language to tell what I felt.

What did I feel? Back then, a longing. Yes, even back then. I wrote about love being the birds and trees and stars, in a place where there was no fear or hate, and ended with the lines "Here I live in a land serene/Alas, it's but a wishful dream." At age ten I already had a Zen-like vision of the world. Perhaps we all do as children. And I hadn't yet started comparing my writing to anyone else's. After all, what would I compare my poems to? I hadn't made a connection between the poems I wrote and the ones in our classroom anthology. Sure, I knew they were related, but I viewed that relationship as similar to lions and house cats, distant relatives. I also hadn't developed the vocabulary for comparison: criticism, it's called, and to this day it can paralyze me. Back then the experience of writing was sheer delight and a sense of connection to something magical, mysterious, and bigger than me: the only thing bigger than me that wasn't scary.

A lot has happened since fifth grade.

For one, I became a teacher. My job is to help people make progress with their writing. Whether through cultivating creativity, getting jump-started, tackling obstacles, rewriting, or publishing, my goal is always the same: to supply people with tools and perspectives to develop, discover, and enjoy more about their writing and what I call the Writing Self, which is the part of you that is awakened by the desire to write.

I wrote my first book, *Room to Write,* to invite people to enter writing creatively, to trust their intuition and discover and use their tendencies, passions, and resistances as fodder for more writing. At that time people seemed to need to free up their innate creative juices and get the words flowing. Since then, at book appearances and during my workshops and writing courses, I've repeatedly had this experience: People thank me for helping them to trust themselves as writers and then ask me how to take the next step.

What do you see as the next step? I ask.

Whether the answer had to do with getting an agent, writing longer works, feeling legitimate, or any of the many other facets of creative writing, the undertone was the same: a sense of longing or unrest about writing. It felt as if each person was saying to me, "Okay, I get the words out, I even trust them sometimes; now what?" This book is my answer.

By continuing to teach and reflect on the evolution of my own Writing Self, I saw another necessity: to cultivate a nourishing writing life. I began to note what made my friends and students seem satisfied and comfortable as writers. I also examined the turning points in my life that led me to feel increasingly fulfilled as a writer. I realized they came about by attending to the balance and flow of all the elements of the Writing Self. To be fulfilled as a writer you have to do more than put words on a page. You have to respect your Writing Self by taking care of all of it.

The writers I know who are passionate and grounded, who truly love and respect their writing life, consciously attend to three aspects of writing that often get short shrift in the heat and excitement of raw creation:

1. Percolation—the process that takes place before a first draft takes shape
2. Revision—the writer's role after the initial draft
3. Going Public—a writer's mission once the writing is done.

This book is for anyone who writes. It will help you explore and shift your relationship to Percolation, Revision, and Going Public so that you can enjoy your place as a writer in the world, and so that you don't use your writing desires to berate yourself. In other words, this is a vehicle to help you realize or maintain balance, flow, and health as a writer, to go for the long burn.

Although this book won't tell you exactly how to get published, in the section on Going Public it offers motives, choices, and encouragement to fulfill your public role as a writer. And even though this book doesn't cover ways to tap into your creativity, in the sections about Percolation and Revision it supplies opportunities and tools for using your creativity both through and beyond a first draft and offers good reasons to be excited about doing it. In a sense, this is your next-step-in-the-process-of-writing companion.

Through defining Percolation, Revision, and Going Public, their nuts and bolts and their fuller meanings, purposes, and importance for your Writing Self, you will examine points in the writing process where writers are prone to imbalances, such as the areas of grasping inspiration, writing daily; working with teachers, joining writing groups; making revision decisions; and the why, when, and how of going public. You'll also see how neglecting Percolation, Revision, and Going Public is the root of many specific writing obstacles.

Everybody experiences the writing process differently. For one person it's more intellectual, for another person it's primarily an emotional experience, for someone else it's foremost an intuitive process. So when you do one of the exercises you may get something different from it than somebody else. There's also a physical aspect to writing, and some people relate to their Writing Self best through engaging their body. I've included several body-mind exercises designed to help you integrate concepts on a physical level. Even if you're more of a cerebral or an emotional writer, I hope you'll try a couple of these activities because their benefit may surprise you. Don't dismiss the effectiveness of the body-mind connection even if at first you feel a little uncomfortable or foolish doing these exercises. Everyone's creative process is also unpredictable. Accordingly, I encourage you to try exercises that may not, on the surface, make complete sense to you. Sometimes we have to do first and understand later.

Recently, a writer friend of mine showed me a magazine article that said marriage is a person's last best hope of growing up. I nodded. It's true of the marriage between writer and writing, too. You are challenged to do exactly what is hard and maybe scary for you. It's part of the point, the reward, the nourishment to meet those challenges. A romance with words isn't enough. The most fulfilling part of the relationship is work. Lifelong love is work and so is a lifelong writing life. As you consider my perspectives and sample the exercises that speak to your Writing Self, you will assemble the techniques and perspectives necessary for you to experience the incredible rewards of the *whole* writing experience, even the challenges—especially the challenges.

One

RESPECT YOUR WRITING

Ultimately, how fulfilled you feel as a writer is in proportion to how much you respect your Writing Self. By respect, I mean the degree to which you accept and appreciate all the ways your writing nourishes you. The reason to cultivate percolation, revision, and going public is really to support your relationship with your writing so that it's dynamic rather than frustrating or depleting. Your Writing Self is an evolving, creative force. If I could give you only one suggestion for nourishing a long and fulfilling writing life, it would be to respect this aspect of it.

Given the ebb-and-flow nature of creativity, respect for our writing is hard for most of us to maintain without some help now and then. When I talk to other writers, students and colleagues alike, we all admit to feeling like fakes sometimes when we say we're writers. Some people will *never* say they're writers because they don't feel legitimate enough. Too many writers I've met have lost their respect for their writing and say they're writers with a note of sadness or anger in their voices.

I don't ask people if they're writers anymore because of the enormous set of expectations wrapped up in that title:

"Do you write?" I ask instead.

"Yes, but . . ." is the answer I hear often, followed by any of the
   following:

I've never been published at all/in the right places/in hardcover.

Only when I have a deadline.

I don't write every day.

I'm not very good at it.

I've never had any formal training.

A very well-respected teacher/writer told me I wasn't very good/
   committed.

I can't write a novel/a screenplay/a poem more than twenty lines
   long.

I never finish anything.

I only keep a journal.

Nobody appreciates how talented I really am.

I can't spell/I never learned proper grammar.

I don't have the time to really devote myself.

I can't get an agent/publisher (I have a terrible agent/publisher).

I don't get reviews/reviews in the important places (I get bad
   reviews).

I call these responses the Confessions. We each keep a few of them
close to our hearts. They are potent; they make us feel better and
worse at the same time, each time we say them. We feel better because
our reasons seem to supply an explanation, a cause for our frustration. We feel worse because the more we speak them, the more we
believe they're true. We assume the Confessions are profound truths
because they inspire strong emotions. But as specific as they may feel
to each of us, they're actually interchangeable. In fact, consider your
reaction to the confessions that don't even pertain to you. If you can't
seem to finish anything, for example, you might feel that a person
who complains he's never been published in hardcover hasn't much to

complain about. If you don't get reviewed in the "important" places, you might be impatient with the confession "I can't find time to write." Or you might feel relieved that you don't have that issue. Or you might experience empathy, remembering back to when that was your problem, too. The Confessions stand like emblems for the set of challenges that are universal to writers. Therefore, once we clear away one reason for feeling "less than" a real writer, a new one will often emerge to take its place. This phenomenon erodes a lot of people's respect for their Writing Self.

The fact is, issues eventually and continually arise for all who write or dream of writing when we realize it isn't enough to get past the fear of filling up the page with words. We also have to balance the amount of energy we devote to the various elements of the writing process. When aspects of our Writing Self are out of alignment, our relationship to writing gets clogged up by our doubts, fears, frustrations, complaints, and confessions. Until we develop our personal set of tools for restoring flow to the creative process, all these issues diminish not only our respect for our writing but our ability to do it.

A Few Words on Writing "Blocks"

The most common sign of an imbalance in your Writing Self is the infamous block, or what I prefer calling a blockage or an obstacle. Obstacles are the thoughts that prevent you from doing an aspect of writing or from enjoying it. They aren't the exclusive problem of beginning writers, either. I know longtime and professional writers who have gone so far with their writing but can't move further. They have their shtick and they get stuck in it.

We don't get stuck in our obstacles because we're stupid or clumsy or bad writers. We get stuck because our focus has narrowed. Having lost sight of the whole writing process, we neglect crucial aspects of it— percolation, revision, and going public. In turn the neglect creates imbalances, stoppages, and obstacles. In the introduction to *Room to Write,* I said that the only true obstacle to writing creatively is a lack of faith that appears as fear and self-judgment. I still believe that faltering faith is at the root of all the types of writer's block. What I notice is that much of what people perceive as obstacles and stoppages is due to being out of alignment with either the percolation, rewriting, or the public aspects of their Writing Self. If you give too much or not enough energy to one or more of them, then the flow of the writing process is disturbed and a blockage occurs.

This is the chiropractic/acupuncture school of writing. I've seen it in my own creative life as well as in other people's. Every time I experience the onset of a blockage, if I look at my relationship with percolation, rewriting, and going public, I usually find one of them is out of sync, causing my Writing Self grief. As I've attended to each of these aspects more consciously over the years, I've found that I experience fewer blocks and move through them more easily. I've seen great shifts in my writing take place as well. Looking at obstacles as readjustment signals instead of a lack of ability is the nourishing and respectful way to relate to your Writing Self.

The Writing Self can be thrown out of alignment by a variety of factors and forces, including negative experiences from the past and neglecting the care and feeding of your Writing Self in the present. However it happens, there isn't an actual writing chiropractor to call. We each make the adjustments we need ourselves as we go along. Those who feel nourished by their writing life are those who have learned how to use their painful writing experiences or challenging obstacles to regain their balance and grow from the difficulties. They're also the ones who know that challenges don't disappear forever, and therefore they have developed coping strategies for when obstacles resurface—as they inevitably do.

Establishing balance between the various elements of writing is awkward at first, especially for those of us who have one or two extreme aspects to our makeup: extremely analytical/emotional/private/scattered/

ambitious, etc. Such extremes carry over to your writing life when, for example, you spend all your time getting words on paper or you become completely obsessed with revision. By itself, awareness of your tendencies isn't enough to restore your writing process. You must make changes. By learning how to nurture all the facets of writing, you learn how to move through obstacles and work with your natural extremes.

Have a Salt Attitude

The first important step to take, whatever your challenges around writing, is to respect them as fuel for your creative process. Think of your writing frustrations and dissatisfactions as being like salt. Basically salt is good. Chemically it's absolutely necessary to maintain the health of our bodies and for us to thrive. Salt deficiency can lead to death. And yet while salt enhances the flavor of many foods, too much of it can ruin a recipe. Salt is used to preserve foods that nourish people in times of need, but the same crystals have been used to torture people when rubbed into an open wound.

Like salt, the challenges that we come up against in our writing life can spoil it or enrich it. Without any obstacles we wouldn't evolve as writers or continue to feel passionate about writing. I would go so far as to say that the challenges our writing presents us with are some of the greatest gifts our writing has to offer. They're invitations to grow as a writer. If you look at the source of your obstacles with the same respect as you see their remedies, you learn to welcome the *blocks* of salt in the written world with a *grain* of salt—the understanding that your obstacles are necessary and life-supporting but that they cause damage unless you have the right attitude toward them. As you examine your relationship to percolation, revision, and going public, try to keep this more respectful salt attitude toward your personal writing challenges.

Body-Mind Exercise

∿ LISTEN TO YOUR BODY

I wish everyone who writes would do this exercise. We tend to house a lot of our most important beliefs about ourselves in our body and voice. Hunched shoulders carry our stress and tight voices contain our anger. When we take a deep breath and relax our body, our emotions and intellect calm down, too. So you can discover your perceptions about writing in your body and voice and use both to help you change your attitudes.

Begin this exercise either standing or sitting in a chair. Say, "I'm a writer." Say it again. Notice the tone in your voice as you say the words. Exaggerate your tone so you can really hear it. Name it: Does your voice sound apologetic, aggressive, questioning?

Now focus on your body. Say, "I'm a writer," in your regular voice and again in the exaggerated voice, but this time also exaggerate your body position. Name it: What is your posture, where are your eyes focused, what are your hands doing, what is the position of your feet, how deep is your breath?

Next, walk around in a large circle or back and forth across the room and say, "I'm a writer," either as you walk or stopping each time you say it. Exaggerate both your body movements and your voice. Notice how you feel. Lie down on the floor and say, "I'm a writer," and let your body move into whatever position it's drawn to. Stay in that position and repeat, "I'm a writer," five or six times. What does it feel like to be in that position? Do you feel relaxed? Confined? Vulnerable? Uncomfortable? Change positions and repeat, "I'm a writer," several times in as many different poses as you want.

Finally, stand in a position that feels grounded, comfortable, and powerful. In an easy, audible voice, say, "I'm a writer," five times. Now move around the room in a joyful way—skip, spin, sway—and say, "I'm a writer," about ten times.

Record in writing your experience of this exercise. Your body can't lie to you. The ways that you hear your voice and feel about the positions of your body reflect the ways you feel about yourself as a writer, even if you aren't intellectually connected to them. You carry these attitudes with you into your creative process, and they either support your Writing Self's growth and sense of fulfillment or hinder it. If your voice sounds defensive and you stick out your chin as you speak the phrase, your body is telling you that you think you have something to prove. Your responses to these physical exercises offer insights about your obstacles as a writer.

The last part of this exercise will help you start to change your attitudes about writing. Your body will remember your new, joyful associations with being a writer, which will help you integrate more nourishing attitudes into your Writing Self as you work to develop them through percolation, revision, and going public. The next time someone asks you what you do, remember your experience of this exercise as you look into their eyes and reply, "I write."

I
PERCOLATION

Work as Nature works, not as men.

RILKE

Everything is gestation and then birthing.

RILKE

Two

THE IMPORTANCE
OF PERCOLATION

Percolation is the process writers go through before actually writing. It's a particular way of paying attention that begins the moment you're inspired. You continue to percolate as you spend time with your inspiration and allow it to develop. This includes everything you do that leads up to a first draft, the time between any two writing sessions, even the time during the breaks you take in a single writing session. Percolation tapers off as you solidify your first inklings in words, but it doesn't end until you're entirely finished with a piece.

At the onset of percolation, inspiration can take several forms. Some people use first thoughts or automatic writing as inspiration. This type of writing without stopping or censoring yourself is a fruitful technique. But relying on only one tool is limiting. Potential pieces of writing are lost to us if we don't notice all the ways we're being inspired, or we ignore inspiration because we're busy with something else at the time.

That passing thought you had as you stepped out of the elevator, the way the sunlight hit your pillow, the instant you saw your son and briefly flashed on an image of him as a peacock, the memories you have when the smell of boiling cabbage wafts past you—these are all inspirations. Out of the random chaos of events something strikes you: a dream, a scrap of conversation, a scent, a scene. It stands out momentarily and gets your attention. Inspiration is an intimate moment of being completely present in the company of something that contains a message. As such, sometimes inspiration can be daunting. I've been struck by material that felt too difficult to take up. I've turned away, refused; but the material eventually returns, in other forms, until I feel ready for it. The more you notice flashes of inspiration, the less you'll need to rely on techniques such as automatic writing to bring out your ideas, and the more you'll trust your own senses.

Once you decide to follow an inspiration's lead, there are lots of ways to percolate. One is to consciously keep company with your idea by repeating it to yourself and noticing the effect. For example, a line pops into your head such as, *What I really remember about John is a single night.* As you say it to yourself over and over you become aware of the range of emotions it brings out, or maybe the character who is speaking the line starts to emerge. Another technique is to percolate about the opposite of your idea to see how it plays off of the original. In the case of John, you might repeat to yourself the line, *What I really remember about John is not even a single night* or *What I really remember about John is a lot more than a single night.* A third technique is to look for connections between your idea and people, places, and situations that are part of your life. For instance, if the line about John came to you while you were house hunting, something about one of the houses you saw or something about your realtor may figure into your emerging piece about John. A related way to percolate is to notice how your idea suggests something to try in your own life. Going back to John, you might percolate for a couple of days by coming up with single events that capture the essence of the people you're closest to. Finally, you can simply coax your idea by taking the time to fully experience your excitement, curiosity, or wonder about it. If you're prone to obsession or you've already given your idea a lot of attention, percolating might be most fruitful if you let the idea steep in the recesses of your mind for a while while you do something else.

However you do it, the point of percolation is to let the little cells of the idea gather, divide, and multiply in order to sustain life and energy outside of your thoughts, to coalesce into something that isn't crushed by written words or blown away by your busy mind. Once the idea has introduced itself, but before you decide to explore it in writing, it needs to take hold and brew in your body and psyche. Something new has stimulated your system. It's full of the potential to grow into a life separate from you. Like any seed, if the idea is forced into the light of day too soon by impatience or expectations, it shrivels. I've lost pieces because I've confused inspiration with ripeness, because I was afraid I'd forget the idea if I didn't get it all down right away, because I made keeping to my writing schedule more important than the writing. After a long time I learned that keeping an idea inside for a while helps me to slow down, adjust my expectations, and respect my ideas.

Edna O'Brien once said, "Writing is like carrying a fetus." Just as a fetus first grows amphibian-like gills and a tail before it takes its final human form, so a piece of writing first needs to develop into a pre-written state in the world of the psyche. Percolation is the incubation time, but there's no standard gestation period like nine months for a human baby or twenty-one days for a chick. You can't predict that it will take six weeks for a short story to grow or twelve minutes for a poem. You might percolate for ten minutes or ten years. One of your Writing Self's roles is to live with your ideas, get to know them, and intuit when they are ready to see the light of words.

One way you can tell an idea is growing is that you notice other events or images in the world or in your memory that connect to your maturing idea. When I was living purely with the idea of writing an essay about making borscht, I saw a relationship between me scavenging my fridge for the ingredients and a mouse in my kitchen foraging for crumbs. That connection ultimately affected the tone of my piece. Another frequent clue for me is when a phrase comes to mind and I find myself repeating it, enjoying the sound and the feel in my mouth. In one instance, I found myself repeating the line, *My daughter washes Buddha's tushie,* and returning to the rhythm and humor of that line, before writing a poem describing my daughter playing on a statue of the Buddha. Perhaps you notice your idea is growing when one scene or character becomes vivid in your mind. These are some of the fruits of percolation.

Imagine the process of percolation as time your idea spends in what I call "the inner city"—the part of the written world that lies within us. Cities are places of convergence where people, cultures, and ideas whirl, swirl, and brush up against one another, creating synergistic moments and intriguing contrasts. While your idea lives in the inner city of your psyche, it becomes infused with divergent energies. The truth is, most writing ideas have been gathering momentum within us for a long time. They surface as inspiration when they grow urgent. In a sense, percolation is the period of time you give to your emotions, intellect, intuition, and imagination to recognize that your idea is now a priority.

So fertile is this period that some writers actually compose their entire first draft during percolation and deliver their poem or story fully realized when they sit down to write. Alice Walker has said that she creates a whole novel in her mind before writing it. For a while, I made short poems in my mind when I was nursing an infant and wrote down the complete poems while she slept. Nevertheless, most of us, most of the time, leave the inner city of percolation with a small parcel of words, an image, a voice that once committed to writing will create the initial momentum necessary to propel a first draft.

I'm not suggesting that every piece you give percolation time to will be easy to write or well written. Even when you've had plenty of time to ruminate on a piece you want to write, it still may have a difficult birth or be small. But taking the time to percolate on an idea will nourish your Writing Self because you are exercising two necessary qualities that a writer needs: the stillness that makes writers able to recognize the extraordinary within the ordinary and the patience it takes to fully realize your ideas. These aren't attributes you must already excel at. They are qualities that you develop through writing. The more attention you pay to percolating, the more still and patient you become.

Once you start to put down words on paper, your idea begins to solidify and become ordered. Then you can affect it as much as it can affect you. You start to form opinions: It's the best idea I've had yet, it's ridiculous, it's too hard, it's been done before, if it isn't a hit I give up. But while the idea floats around in your psyche, without form, you are enveloped in the beauty of not knowing what it will be. You're open. You're vulnerable. You're stargazing: now finding the Dipper, now losing it again. You are inside creation.

The closest experience to this state I can name is lying in a meadow and watching clouds as your imagination continuously transforms them into creatures and objects. Try this sometime in order to get reacquainted with the process. It feeds your creativity. In the same way, even if the piece that you begin winds up fizzling out or disappointing you, your Writing Self has been nurtured by the percolation process.

There's one more benefit from giving this type of attention to your idea. Your Writing Self has more time to fall in love with the idea before criticizing it. You focus on the idea in traffic, on your daily walk, in your staff meeting, maybe even while you're making love. For some the idea becomes an obsession, while for others it just peeks through here and there during the day. Either way, it's this growing feeling of love or commitment that will help you to take the next step of completing a first draft.

Resistance Is Futile

If percolation is really such an essential element of the writing process, why do we resist it? For one thing, many people feel impatient about it. It requires a state of stillness we are not accustomed to. For another thing, sometimes being as free-form in our writing process as we are during percolation creates anxiety. Without our ideas firmly planted in writing, we feel dizzy and out of control. Also, most of us learn to accomplish our goals by taking tangible actions, especially when it comes to writing. We count words, pages, chapters. As a result, even writing teachers feel compelled to provide students with word-generating activities to get their uncensored words out or to help them avoid procrastination.

Procrastination is a myriad of excuses for not writing. Sometimes we confuse it with percolation because in both cases we're not producing visible words. The similarities between the two make us uncomfortable; but *percolation isn't procrastination*. We need the energy percolating supplies to our ideas. The psyche is at work. Our senses are attuned inward. We're feeding our idea.

Another of our discomforts with percolation is that in the written world it is unmappable territory. We can't predict where it will lead us or how we will get there. I think of the percolation time of writing as being similar to the time it takes to adjust to the climate, time zone, and culture of another land.

Percolation is one of the most elusive aspects of writing. It happens behind the scenes, under cover, in the dark recesses. It also happens in line at the grocery store, in the shower, in the middle of lunch. For the same reason, it's something we *can* take for granted because, like breathing, it happens whether or not we give attention to it. But just like breathing, when we concentrate on percolation, it nourishes us more fully.

In this way percolation is a fundamental facet of the yogic aspect of writing. In yoga practice we always begin class by paying attention to our breath, and we use it to center ourselves within and between poses, because breathing into the poses is how we intensify, advance, and learn from them. We experience the same benefits for our Writing Self when we begin by mindfully percolating: Our focus intensifies, our idea advances, and we learn from whatever we write. Breathing is to yoga as percolation is to writing in one more way as well. Like breathing, percolation isn't an exclusively inner process. When we breathe we take in *and* we let out. Similarly, percolation includes external processes that help prepare what swirls and whirls inside us for the written word: practices such as daily writing, distillation, and reading, which we'll look at closely in the next chapter.

Practice

⌒ PLUGGING INTO PERCOLATION

This is a tool for consciously entering the percolation process. It eases you into it without the pressure of having to produce something, like a page of writing, afterward. Use this practice for any of the reasons you want to connect to percolating, including: it's been a long while since you've given yourself time to percolate, or it's an uncomfortable or unfamiliar experience you want to acclimate yourself to, or you like to begin percolating with a focusing activity.

To connect to the experience of percolation, spend time watching clouds. It's best if you lie down, but sitting comfortably will do. Notice how the clouds constantly transform into different shapes and how their appearance suggests small scenes and dramas to you. If you live in a cloudless climate or where they rarely form distinct shapes, try stargazing instead by inviting your imagination to make up its own constellations.

The most intensive way to use this tool is to cloud-watch for one hour during three separate sessions over a two-week period. In the first hour don't be surprised if you mostly run up against your resistances to percolating, like feeling agitated or nervous about keeping track of the time. By the third session your psyche will be more comfortable in this state. Remember two things during this practice.

1. It doesn't matter whether you find yourself making up several dramas and images from the cloud forms or you end up weaving one narrative from them.
2. Unlike meditation, with cloud watching, rather than trying to clear your mind of thoughts, you're actually opening your mind for images to visit you.

Depending on your reasons for doing this practice, you can modify it to suit your needs. Twenty-minute cloud-watching sessions are good for getting back into a percolation mode, while regular ten-minute sessions work well as a focusing practice before writing or as small steps for those who have a hard time reveling in such a receptive state as percolation. Any way you choose to do this exercise, make sure you won't be interrupted.

∼ EMPTY SPACE

Percolation can feel elusive and intangible for those of us who need to "see results." How can you invest more of your time in the process if you don't appreciate the fruits of doing it enough to cultivate it? This is a tool that adjusts the way we look at creative writing to include literally seeing percolation. This alternate way of seeing not only illuminates the rewards of percolation, it also tunes you into the subtle results of percolation present in all creative output.

Do this practice in two stages, first with a non-writing medium such as painting, music, or dance, and second, in relation to writing. First, choose a painting to look at and instead of concentrating on the objects or images, focus on the shapes of the space around them, what's often referred to as negative space. You may want to start by gazing at the actual objects in the painting for a time and then slowly shifting your attention to the shapes formed by the spaces between the objects. Or listen to a piece of music, giving all your attention to the silences and pauses instead of the instruments. You'll probably have to hear the piece several times before you can keep your attention on the quiet parts. Or watch a dance performance so that you're looking at the shapes made by the spaces between the dancers instead of looking directly at the dancers. It's frustrating to try this at a live perform-ance. A dance video is better. You can watch it once in the traditional way and view it a second time my way.

Regardless of the medium you choose, the point is to appreciate how the pauses or spaces enrich creative work through the anticipa-tion, relief, rest, etc., that they provide. I think of the empty space as the breath of a piece and as the manifestation of the percolation that went into its creation.

When we give our attention to the empty spaces in writing, it's like seeing percolation in its physical form. For the second half of this practice, select a poem and read it twice. The first time, take in the meaning of the words. The second time, concentrate on how the white space between stanzas, lines, and even between the words shapes both the poem and your experience of it. Look for how the white space supplies suspense, rhythm, or time to linger a moment longer with an image. Taking the time to acknowledge the influence of the white space adds a whole other dimension to how you experience the poem—the percolative dimension. Of course with prose writing we have to put spaces between words and paragraphs even when we don't percolate. But there is a stronger synergy between the words and the empty spaces when the empty spaces are infused with percolation time. It's one of the subtle aspects of writing that makes the difference between a good piece and a wonderful piece.

∿ PERCOLATE WHILE CLEANING YOUR BATHROOM BOWL

There was once a TV commercial for a cleaning product that showed a series of women involved in leisure activities. The camera would zoom in on each woman, and in a conspiratorial tone each would confess, "I'm cleaning my bathroom bowl!" The idea was that the cleaning product cleaned your toilet bowl while you were off having fun. In my commercial for a fulfilled Writing Self, I'd show people cleaning their toilet bowl. The camera would zoom in for a close-up, and each person would proudly proclaim, "I'm percolating!" Although I usually don't promote people doing two things at once, percolating is an exception. I encourage writers to consciously percolate when they're doing the very activities they do while grumbling, *I'd rather be writing.* Percolation is an aspect of writing that there's always time to do.

To experience your capacity to percolate under any circumstances, pick one task you dread doing this week, such as paying bills, and while you're doing it, consciously take some time to call to your mind an idea you want to write about. While you're paying the bills, look for the ways it suggests material for your writing idea. Ask yourself some related questions, for example: How do my characters deal with money or other kinds of debt? Another way to make a connection between the task at hand and your writing project is to reflect on some aspect of the nature of the task. For instance, does the repetitive nature of paying bills hint at a way to structure a scene you're writing? Jot down your ideas in a writer's journal to refer to when you start a first draft. You can use this percolation technique anytime you have to do a chore you dislike, or you can pick one chore a week and use it as deliberate percolation time.

If your writing time is being eaten up during special circumstances such as a period of transition or holiday time, this percolation technique will help you stay connected to your writing project until the rhythm of your life is restored. The technique is also an invaluable one for writers who write in cycles, what I call writing seasons, meaning writing only during particular periods of the year, such as over the summer. During your "off season" you can use a predetermined chore as deliberate percolation time so that when your writing season begins, you're ripe with ideas.

Body-Mind Exercise

∼ PERCOLATE

It's challenging to invest time in percolation because of the amorphous nature of working with strands of ideas and bits and pieces of thoughts before writing them down. In a later chapter I call your writer's journal your psyche's inner-city dump. To experience the value of percolation before committing to doing it as part of your regular writing process, I invite you to try percolating in a visceral, concrete way by visiting a literal dump site. Walk around for at least a half hour studying the objects you pass by. Look at them in the way you would look at art pieces in a museum—allowing yourself time to experience your emotions and reactions to the pieces. Take home two unrelated items that you had a reaction to and put them next to each other near where you write. If you can't get to a dump but you still want to try this exercise, browse a garage or rummage sale for two unrelated objects. For two weeks look at them for five minutes before you write. By examining them regularly before you write, you'll be able to notice how your experience of the objects changes over time through percolation. You might realize subtle ways the objects are related to each other. Your feelings about one or both of the objects might change over time. You might begin to see a connection between the objects and what you're writing. For a few days you might feel totally bored and irritated with the objects. If that happens, stick with this exercise anyway. At the end of two weeks, take a few minutes to write about how your experience of the objects changed and decide for yourself if the time you invested in percolating reaps enough intriguing results for you to incorporate it into your regular writing process.

Three

READ

Reading is crucial writer's fuel. It is a time-honored means of immersing yourself in the receptive state that percolating is all about. Reading nourishes your writing because it exercises your imagination and receptivity, fills your psyche with rhythms and patterns of language different from your own, and takes you out of your daily life and routine perspectives. Reading is part of the percolation process because you feed your Writing Self in all these ways without creating writing.

Reading exercises many of the same imaginative muscles as writing. Using these muscles in a slightly different way tones them for when we write. It's a bit like exercising the opposing tricep muscles in your arm after working your biceps. Reading contributes to the balance of the Writing Self just as a well-planned workout keeps the whole arm fit. So many people spend more time watching movies than reading. But screenplay writers notwithstanding, for writers the more active experience of reading is of greater benefit to the Writing Self than the relatively passive act of watching films or television.

Reading is the conduit to your Writing Self's lineage and ancestry. Being receptive to your writing ancestors and siblings connects what you are writing vertically through time and horizontally across the present. Learning from the writings of others is a legitimate and necessary form of mentorship. There's no way to underestimate how this connection subtly adds depth and dimension to your own words.

Even so, it's not unusual to come across a book and think, Oh no, that was my idea, now I can't write my book. Or, No one will want to read my book now because the concept has already been done. Some writers feel that reading compromises their originality or influences them in other negative ways. I find this perspective self-limiting. I look at authors who write on a topic similar to mine as a brother or a grandmother to my own book idea. Just as you share a gene pool with your relatives that can cause you to have several strikingly similar traits, it's very likely that you share some writing ideas with your writing relatives and ancestors. Similarities between you and your blood relatives are not a reason to abandon your goals. Discovering overlaps between your work and another writer's isn't either. Instead, it encourages you to sort out the facets of the subject you can add to.

Often what ignites our urge to write in the first place is what we read. Many people begin to write because they've been inspired by someone else's writing. We want to join the conversation from the other side of the page. Reading is one way to begin meaningful dialogue with yourself or others. It is a first receptive step toward taking action in the world as a writer or a citizen. You read something and it makes you want to respond in word or deed.

But just as some people read *rather* than take action in the world, sometimes writers read rather than write. Lulled by receiving the constant stimulation of ideas and images that reading supplies, we get distracted from creating our own. If this sounds like you, limit your reading when you're writing a draft and indulge in it freely when you're percolating. I know a novelist, for example, who reads poetry only while writing the first draft of a novel but who reads voraciously and indiscriminately when the draft is complete. Another novelist I know read every nineteenth-century novel she could get her hands on that took place in the Windy City when writing the first draft of a historical set in Chicago. She used reading to immerse her Writing Self in the universe of her novel. Once she finished writing her draft, she broadened her reading horizons so that it was once again a receptive and percolative experience.

Thomas Moore describes a book as a metaphorical temple, "a place of relief from daily existence." Reading immerses us in a timelessness that, like a temple, rejuvenates our psyche by fully engaging it in a world completely outside the details of our lives. When you read, you're a human *being* because you receive the written world. When you write you're a human *doing* because you contribute to the written world. For those who don't write, reading in itself is enough of a fulfilling relationship to the written world. As a writer, reading is fuel that your Writing Self uses to percolate.

Practice

∾ R & R : READ AND RECEIVE

When we immerse ourselves in reading, not only do specific passages or ideas stimulate us, but on a subtler level we soak in the material, whether it be the perspective of the writer or her sentence patterns. One consequence of writing is that it causes you to read in two distinct ways: as a student of writing and as a receptive reader. When I read as a student of writing, I'm actively trying to learn something from reading that will help me write. I might pay special attention to the author's style or the techniques she uses to develop an idea. I often read with a pencil in hand to mark or underline passages and ideas I want to explore in my own writing. Reading this way is nurturing because of how stimulating it is.

When I read as a receptive reader, I put my pencil down along with my agenda. I read to *experience* the author's style and ideas. If I reread a passage, it's purely for the pleasure it gave me the first time or to be sure I've grasped the concept it contains. In this more receptive state I'm in percolation mode. Without a specific mission, my Writing Self floats, weightless, in a sea of words, images, and ideas, free from self-conscious motives. I find that if I don't deliberately decide which kind of reading I'm going to do, in the midst of a book, I flip-flop between reading as a student of writing and as a receptive reader.

It nourishes your creativity and your percolation process to spend some regular time exclusively as a receptive reader. To do it, deliberately set aside receptive reading time and material. Start with a minimum of fifteen minutes. Pick a time, like right after a writing session or just before bed. It will help you settle in to receptivity if you can ritualize your reading by choosing a location, a particular, comfortable place to sit, and perhaps a soothing beverage to sip. If you can't create such a conducive environment in your life, then do your best with what you have: Read when you're alone in the bathroom, during your bus ride to work, or during one cycle of laundry.

Next, choose reading material that is least likely to tempt you to start taking notes or kibitzing. Some people reserve a genre such as science fiction, poetry, or newspapers. Other people reread favorite works. I read something challenging for me, such as a novel like James Joyce's *Finnegan's Wake,* a nonfiction like Stephen Hawking's *A Brief History of Time,* or an epic poem like Spenser's *The Faerie Queene.* With reading like this I don't attempt to understand every word or concept on an intellectual level. Instead I enjoy and absorb the texture of the sentences, or the voice of the characters, or the tone of the book. Sometimes, to prevent myself from actively reading as a student of writing, rather than approach a book from start to finish, I randomly dip into it.

If you tend to read to avoid writing instead of to support your Writing Self, these suggestions for receptive reading are also excellent tools to help you limit the amount you read.

Four

DON'T WRITE
EVERY DAY

I know that it's practically heresy to encourage writers not to write, but sometimes for all the good reasons there are to write daily, there are as many equally good reasons not to write daily. The Writing Self, like the physical self, needs more than one kind of care. If you exercise regularly but eat poorly, claiming you don't have time to make healthy meals because you're busy working out, I'd say, eat a little better and exercise a little less. Self-care is about balance. If you came to my workshop and told me you have fourteen first-draft stories but no finished ones, I'd say create less, rewrite more. Balance is important in all realms of life, and the writing life is no exception.

It's not surprising, therefore, that a fair amount of people's unhappiness or dissatisfaction with their writing life develops from imbalances. Maybe you're bitter about not being published. In this case your ability to share your work is out of balance with your ability to produce it. Or perhaps you're discouraged because you've been so caught up in rewriting your memoir that you haven't begun writing anything new for six years. You've lost your equilibrium between revision and the creation of new material. One way to maintain the balance of your Writing Self is *not* to write every day. Not writing allows time for percolation to take place, gives your creativity time to replenish, and gives you the distance from your writing to gain perspective on it.

I don't always write every day, and often others breathe a palpable sigh of relief when I tell them this. There are, in fact, successful writers who *never* write every day because they find it interferes with maintaining a balanced writing life. Even Natalie Goldberg, the queen of writing practice, admits she no longer writes every day. For everything there's a time and place. Even rest. Particularly rest.

The truth is, though, that we live in a culture with a suspicious attitude regarding rest. Despite the fact that a regular Sabbath is built into many spiritual traditions, we've developed a mistrust of our desire for rest, and as a result we're often at a loss for how to experience it. We know exactly how to work; we often don't really know how to relax. Why? Maybe we think we're going to miss out on some experience or accomplishment, maybe we're scared of feeling emptiness or pain, maybe we've confused doing with being. My grandmother used to say, "I can rest when I'm dead." What's your attitude toward rest?

It's relatively simple to learn *how* to rest from your writing as long as you've first accepted rest as a necessity. Without rest, we become tired and so does our writing. It's like the story of *The Red Shoes,* in which the young girl who loves to dance is destroyed by that love when she puts on a pair of shoes that cause her to dance without being able to stop. We are ingenious creatures; we can use anything, even our greatest gifts, like writing, to hurt ourselves if we aren't mindful about *how* we use what we possess.

One way to rest from writing is to engage in experiences in which you receive rather than produce. Listening to music is a way to rest (as long as you don't clean the house simultaneously). Reading is restful if you can do it for pleasure and enrichment instead of as a kibitzer, looking for tips for your own writing.

To replenish the Writing Self, I encourage people to rest through each of their five senses. My ways of doing this include floating around in a swimming pool (touch), eating a cheese-and-cracker snack using a different mustard for each one (taste), and deeply inhaling a cup of herbal tea as I drink it (smell). Poet Natasha Sajé finds periods of silent walking essential to her percolation process. The physical experience of the rhythm of walking opens her thoughts.

Another type of rest from daily writing is simply doing the other work you normally do: gardening, parenting, programming, plumbing. Nobody just writes. Even poet Emily Dickinson, who rarely left her house, would cook, clean, and interact with family members on a regular basis. Many people, including me, complain about having to do other work besides writing. Why can't I make my whole living by my art? we moan. Through my experience of the creative arts as a writer first and a choreographer and visual artist second, I've come to view all creativity as an extension of the world, an act of making love with it. And it's impossible to make love with the world separate from it.

During a repertory class I took with choreographer Kei Takei, about fifty of us were learning a section of her dance "Wheat Fields." The piece included a long, repetitive movement sequence that suggested gathering up piles of wheat and throwing them over our shoulders into a bag. After many tries at having us achieve the quality of movement she was after and watching us fail to grasp it each time, Kei sat us down on the gymnasium floor and looked at us with something like compassion mixed with confusion. She quietly explained that the rural people in her region of Japan *liked* work. A little embarrassed, we all nodded, got up, and did the movement correctly. My understanding of all work in relation to creative work was forever changed.

Poet Robert Graves points out how intimately our earliest examples of writing are related to work: The oldest English poem, *Beowulf,* is written in lines that include a break every two beats because that was the rhythm that coincided with the Vikings' rowing their boats across the sea. Homer wrote the lines of the *Iliad* to contain three beats followed by two beats, mimicking the call and response of women and men as they worked in the fields. In all these ways, doing our other work is a wellspring for what we write and how we write.

Besides helping us maintain our balance and remember to rest, not writing daily also guards against our own unreasonable demands on ourselves. Earlier, I wrote about having lost some pieces of writing by feeling pressured to write daily and so starting a piece before it was ready to be put in words. Overtaxing new ideas is like expecting a toddler to have steady balance the first time he walks, or presuming that if he took a few steps yesterday, he should take even more today. You'd never be such a taskmaster to your child. You wouldn't think of diminishing or discouraging him in this way. But have you ever expected too much too fast of your Writing Self? The pressure of daily writing can turn against you by giving your critical self permission to interfere with the organic development of a piece of writing. If your critical self shows up too early and comes on too strong, its unreasonable demands rob you of the most basic food necessary for writing: pleasure.

The Pleasure Principle

To write daily or not to write daily; if that is the question, may you make your decision without feeling as haunted as Shakespeare's Hamlet. Keep in mind the Pleasure Principle. Writing is supposed to give you pleasure. That doesn't preclude its being hard work or temporarily frustrating, or tapping into a reservoir of difficult emotions and memories. Pleasure in this sense isn't the exclusive realm of what's comfortable. Rather, because of the challenges of writing, at some level you want to feel connected to a sense of excitement, anticipation, urgency, wonder, gratitude, reverence, or downright playfulness and genuine joy as you go along. If you don't, you probably need to walk away from putting words down on paper or screen for a while. Not forever. Not until you have more time or feel all better: just long enough to reestablish your connection to the spirit of writing.

Conversely, sometimes people reconnect *through* writing daily, especially if they haven't written for a long time, or if fear of the material that they're dealing with has derailed their sense of purpose. When you're feeling disconnected from the pleasure of writing, it's a good time to experiment with both ways of regaining it. Start by writing daily for a couple of weeks. If you dread it or find yourself in a morass of self-criticism that gets stronger or more persistent as you write, you're probably rehearsing your negativity rather than exorcising it. Give yourself a two-week break from writing anything at all and use the time to nourish yourself in other, more percolative ways. You'll know you're reconnecting to the pleasure of writing again when you start to feel surges of excitement or curiosity about a writing idea and the self-critical chatter in your mind doesn't numb the anticipation.

Identity Dependency

When you write daily, sometimes your identity as a writer can become dependent on it. What I mean by this is that you feel legitimate or worthy as a writer only when you're producing words on the page or the screen. Granted, this probably isn't the worst dependency to have. But you need to know you're a writer and feel good about your Writing Self even when pen isn't to paper or fingers aren't to keypad because, as life happens, you will find yourself in periods when you're unable to write. During these periods you don't want to be inundated by all the self-critical messages about your writing identity that you've been staving off by writing. You already want to be secure about the wherewithal of your Writing Self so that when you are able to write again you aren't trying to validate yourself as a writer at the same time.

If you've begun to sense that you're writing daily because you're *afraid* not to, then stop writing for a while and explore the feeling of what happens when you stop. Do you feel guilty for not writing or disapproving or contemptuous of yourself? Then it's time for you to challenge those attitudes by strengthening your relationship to the processes of percolating, revising, and sharing—back to the process, not the proof of your accomplishment.

Practice

∼ REVISITING REST

Before deciding whether or not to take a break from writing for a while, take time to notice and then write about your attitude toward rest. Begin by journaling about the following questions: Do you feel rest is an earned or a given right? Why? Do you rest to live or live to rest? What was the attitude toward rest in your family as a child and in your workplace as an adult?

If you find your beliefs about rest, in general, are rigid or negative, you need to develop ways to shift them before you stop writing for a while. Otherwise, not writing will only cause you more stress and discomfort. One suggestion to help shift your relationship to rest is to pick an example of rest from the natural world that inspires you to change your critical perspective and use Nature's example as a reminder of the new attitude toward rest that you're cultivating.

When I did this I chose a flowering cactus. I left it on my writing desk as it blossomed. Then I took its picture in full bloom. Once the blooms were spent, I put the photograph beside the plant on my desk. At that point, each time I sat to write, I glanced at the photo. This practice helped me relax when I took days or weeks away from my writing. To this day, a flowering cactus reminds me of the nourishment that resting from writing provides my Writing Self. Whatever aspect of Nature you choose will become your own private talisman against negative messages about rest.

∽ WORK TO REST

I used to fret a lot about not having enough time to write. I developed resentment about doing mundane chores. Eventually, my resentment began to spill into my feelings about teaching writing, too. I'd lost touch with one of my own basic beliefs—in whatever form the task that's in front of us appears, there's a way that it nurtures what we most love to do. I was able to let go of my resentment by consciously looking for the connections between the other work I did and my writing. With my new perspective, weeding the garden was also a lesson about revising a poem. Cooking was a percolation practice. Whatever topic about writing that I was teaching turned out to be helpful to the current writing project I was working on. As a result, I not only experienced how my other work fed my writing, I also realized how *necessary* my other work was to writing. The analogies I made between writing and my other work were clues about the direction for me to focus on when I did have writing time.

When someone feels overwhelmed by trying to write and do all the other kinds of work she does, I suggest this exercise: On the bottom of a piece of paper, draw a stick figure of yourself with your arms raised above you. Fill up the rest of the paper with phrases that name the things you do; for me it includes parenting, writing, teaching, yoga, walking, acupuncture. Draw a circle around each one. Don't forget to include writing! Take a good look at this illustration of everything you do. Now draw a line to connect each circle that feeds your Writing Self to your writing circle. Write a word or phrase along the line connecting the two circles that states what the connection is. On my drawing, for instance, I connected my household chores circle with my writing circle and wrote: "[household chores are] practice with the repetitive attention it takes to write." With a little reflection and a bit of creative connecting, you'll discover that most of the work you do supports some aspect of your writing. From this exercise, many people develop a more relaxed attitude about the relationship between the other things they do and their writing time. They also start to use the other things they do as a source for percolating about what to concentrate on when they are writing.

Body-Mind Exercise

∾ REST

Resting is more than just stopping what you're doing. Rest is also a time of replenishing yourself, of receiving what is nurturing and restorative. As a way of resting from writing on both these levels, spend time each day this week involved in at least one refilling activity for one of your five senses. For instance: listen to thirty minutes of music (sound); use your lunch hour to people-watch or look at old photos (sight); eat a favorite food slowly and intentionally (taste); surround yourself with a smell you love (burn incense, sit in a bakery for a half hour, walk by the ocean); instead of going for a twenty-minute walk, go for a twenty-minute "touch," meaning, spend the same time you'd walk in the park, for example, touching everything you can—the benches, trees, leaves, swings. If you can't fit all your senses into one week, then do two senses a week or one a week, and don't write on those days. When you are ready to write again, mentally recall the experience of one of your replenishing activities before you begin. It will help get your writing juices flowing.

Five

DISTILLATION: CATCHING THE SPIRIT

The first phase of percolation, ruminating internally, is about letting your idea build by containing it. Distillation is the next step of letting your idea out. The dictionary defines "distill" as to let fall, to subject to transformation, to extract the essence of, to appear slowly in small quantities. In writing terms, distillation is the initial step of putting your idea into words. Distilling actually occurs throughout the evolution of a piece of writing, though it usually begins early in the creative process with a few notations.

Once you've percolated enough on an idea to connect it to memories or other associations, then you're ready to turn the idea into parcels of words. In distillation mode, you write down words just as a toddler goes for a walk—more interested in what you discover along the way than in where you're going. During distillation you aren't as attached to your words as you are when you compose a first draft. You follow your idea in a manner that's more fluid, more open, more meandering. There's a sense of mystery and excitement about what you're writing down. That's distillation.

Journals

A widely practiced distilling technique is the use of journals. A writer's journal isn't the same thing as a traditional journal. It's a genre in its own right, a place for self-exploration and for recording personal journeys. Material from a traditional journal can inspire you to write a story, an essay, or a poem, but it's not the journal's main purpose.

A writer's journal, however, is where you distill ideas. You use it to jot down scraps of conversation or a dream, paste a news item that affected you, or jam for a few pages about a topic that sparks your heart and mind. A writer's journal isn't even necessarily a bound book. You can use whatever works for your lifestyle. Writer Anne Lamott carries around index cards in her pocket so she can make notes anywhere, anytime. While a traditional journal is a progression or an unfolding, a writer's journal is more of a collage or a laboratory.

The great artist Louise Nevelson built her first riveting sculptures out of what she distilled from dump sites. When fit together, the lone balusters, cornices, and pieces of door molding Nevelson found become capable of evoking emotions and stories that range from joyful to terrifying. But she had to collect the pieces first before she could combine them. We do the same when we distill our ideas by writing them in a journal. Just as Nevelson's dump contained fragments, what you've distilled into a journal does not, at first, amount to a complete piece of writing.

A writer's journal is the best distilling tool if you're the kind of writer who gets inspired by several ideas at once. By keeping track of them in the journal, your psyche doesn't get overwhelmed. I use my writing journal to go between percolating and distilling when I get several ideas for essays at the same time. I jot down a phrase in my journal for each idea so I don't lose track of any of them as I percolate on and distill each one. When one essay idea occurs by itself, I just let it percolate in my mind awhile. Then when I have a couple of concepts about what I want to include, or I've formed a first line, I write it in my journal. After that, I let the essay percolate a bit more, distilling what surfaces. When I'm finished distilling, I write a first draft. But even as I work on a first draft, I will often go through my writing journal to see if distilled fragments from past pages relate to anything else in my current essay. One extra benefit of a writer's journal is that it makes you feel more relaxed about your writing in a way that a first draft can't, because it's a no-pressure place to begin to put your ideas into words.

A second way some writers use their journal as a distilling tool is to support their identity as writers. My writing journal is dappled with a running commentary about such topics as what I've discovered as I write, how the discovery connects to other aspects of my life, what writing challenges I'm facing, how the project I'm currently working on is going. In her excellent book *Writing As a Way of Healing,* Louise DeSalvo stresses the importance of keeping what she calls a process journal while writing about difficult life experiences. She calls such a journal a place of "witnessing the creative process and oneself as a writer." I do this witnessing throughout my writing journal, so I call my entries about writing "process passages." Process passages distill your idea of your Writing Self. By recording your writing process—

> *Today I nailed down a confusing section by explaining it aloud to my parakeet. With a lot of my stories I guess I gain clarity by talking them through.*

—you establish a strong connection to how you write by giving it a voice. The more you know about your Writing Self, the more secure you become in yourself as a writer.

One Size Does Not Fit All

Despite the advantages of distilling in a journal, there are plenty of successful writers who never use them. These writers use other distilling tools, or they skip distillation altogether by percolating and then composing a draft in their mind or the moment they sit down to write it. Nichola, who is trained as a journalist and writes for a living, never distills material before writing a nonfiction piece. She jokes about going from percolation to distilling—"coffee to whiskey," she calls it. But she also allows that distillation could be a part of her process when she gets back to fiction writing someday. A musician, Rob distills writing the way he composes. From percolating, he extracts a mood or a single word. Once it's distilled, he develops a first draft by building around it as he writes. My friend Bill uses his dreams as a distilling tool for all his short stories. He doesn't keep a dream journal; he just wakes up, goes to his computer, and writes what he's dreamed as a first draft. If he needs to do research about a part of the dream to flesh out the story, he does it that day or makes a note in the margins to look it up later. Other distillation tools include brainstorming, making outlines, and note taking, particularly if you're writing a piece that requires research. Even talking about your idea and either recording yourself or writing down key phrases as you speak is a method of distilling ideas into words.

A more structured and formal way to shepherd your ideas before writing a first draft is a book proposal. Especially when you're setting out to write a longer piece, a book proposal has the potential to be more than a tool for selling the idea to the business world of writing. It's a distillation technique.

After percolating about the idea for my book *Room to Write,* my first distilling tool was to write ten pages to test out my excitement about the project and my feeling for writing it. I sent the best of those pages and a short letter describing my idea to several agents and editors.

Two contacted me and asked to see a proposal. At first, the prospect of having to write it overwhelmed me. But I found that articulating my idea, what was unique about it, why it was valuable, who I thought might buy it, why I was qualified to write it, actually helped solidify it for my Writing Self.

Writing that proposal supplied me with new enthusiasm, energy, and shape for my vision. It's been the case ever since, with each proposal I've written, and I now use a version of proposal writing as a distillation tool for all my longer work. I'll shift from percolating about a project to writing an overview describing why I want to write the piece, its purpose, scope, and how I imagine I will structure it. Then I describe the people I think would be interested in it. Next, I write about how it's different from other pieces about the same topic, and then I make up short chapter summaries on all the subjects I think I might include. Finally, as an affirmation of my Writing Self, I write down why I'm a great person to write the piece. When I'm done, I have an outline, a vision, material to begin with, and some confidence in my ability to bring my idea into the written world.

The purpose of any form of distillation is to usher your ideas into words that are charged with your inspiration but are still relatively free from your harsh judgments about them. By taking the time to distill, you also create essential material to return to in case you get stuck in the midst of a first draft.

Practice

∽ DARING TO DISTILL

In this practice you experience both the process of distillation and the rewards in one week by using a piece you've already written to work from. Choose a fairly short piece you've finished. Reread it and extract one idea from it by underlining a word or phrase that captures the idea. In a meditation I was writing on caring for aging parents, I extracted the idea of experiencing it as a sacrifice. Let the idea return to your percolating psyche by repeating the phrase to yourself five times and writing it down on a separate sheet of paper. Post it in your writing area. I worked with the single word "sacrifice." For one week, spend ten minutes a day journaling about the idea. At the end of the week, reread your journal entries and notice what new perspectives you have about the idea. After journaling about sacrifice for a week, I began to understand that sacrifice was also about gaining something better than what I thought I was losing. Without having gone through this distilling process, I would have missed this significant point altogether.

∾ DISTILLING LONG WORKS

If you're percolating about a longer project, something book-length, for instance, it helps to use a distilling process that is more structured because you're working with a great many more ideas at once. In the beginning of such a project, the purpose of distillation is to help you create an outline or a scaffold to come back to and build upon. For certain long projects, such as historical fiction or a nonfiction project that requires gathering facts and information, you may want to hold off on this method of distillation until you've finished your first round of research and note taking.

Here's how you write a distillation book proposal. Spend no more than two pages describing what your book idea will be about, its purpose (or why you want to write it), its scope, and how you imagine you'll develop it (i.e., using interviews, anecdotes, exercises, historical info, etc.). If you're working on fiction, this will be where you include a summary of the plot. If you're the type of fiction writer whose plots evolve as you write, it's fine for your summary to be very brief and sketchy. Next, spend no more than a page writing about who you think will want to read your book and why. You don't have to be right about the audience for your project in this section. The point is simply to muse about it a little. Feel free to be humorous if you like: My romance novel will appeal to twice-divorced, Smith & Hawken–shopping, vegan office managers. In a third section, write no more than a page on how your book may be different from works about the same topic. Again, you're only speculating for the purpose of gathering your thoughts. In the fourth section of your proposal, write a one- or two-paragraph summary of each chapter you imagine. In fiction, your summary may be as brief and vague as, "Something shocking happens to the main character," or "By now the conflict is crystal clear." Finally, write up to a page explaining why you're the perfect person to write this book.

By distilling your project in this form of a book proposal before starting a first draft, you pour your ideas into a container that's easily accessible as you write. Keep your proposal available as you work on a first draft. It's your reminder of the spirit of your writing project, and it's the record of your initial goals. I continually refer to my proposal through all drafts of a book manuscript. It is the direct line back to my original thoughts and intuitions, which are often my best ideas, and they're two things that can get buried in piles of research and rewrites.

Six

WRITE EVERY DAY

As a percolation technique, writing daily energizes your creative process. Some writers generate new writing every day to collect their ideas. They sit down and write for a set amount of time or until they've completed a predetermined number of pages. What they write isn't polished, but they put words on the page. Before starting a first draft, writing every day combines distilling with percolating out loud, so to speak.

By repeatedly writing a set number of pages a day, over time you learn how to think in writing, instead of forming an idea in your mind first and then writing about it. It's handy to know how to think in writing. You avoid getting blocked by the leap from thoughts to written words. As long as you're thinking, you can always write something. That way, instead of forming your ideas about the similarities between kayaking and marriage before you start writing, you think it through in writing.

Daily writing gives you a strong sense of accomplishment, too. Spiritual seekers and writers both know how important it is to concentrate on process instead of result, but there's no denying how terrific it feels to follow through on a commitment. Daily writing gives you the confidence that you are, in fact, a writer: As Aristotle said, we are what we repeatedly do.

A third gift of writing daily is that it ferrets out the subtler ways that self-criticism blocks your Writing Self. You may be quite familiar with the more obvious taunting that arises in your mind as you write, such as, My writing is stupid/terrible/a waste of time. Over a sustained period of regular writing, more latent complaints crystallize: I'm being foolish again/What if my mother saw this?/It's not as good as yesterday's work. When you're aware of these slier litanies, it helps you manage them during all phases of writing. For his daily writing practice, the poet William Stafford woke at 4 A.M. every day and wrote at least one poem. When an interviewer asked him how he dealt with writer's block, Stafford replied that he never experienced it. If he had trouble getting started or felt stuck in the midst of a poem, he lowered his standards, he said. Stafford's daily practice helped him to see below the surface. He learned that often it is a set of standards that blocks writing, not, for example, a lack of material.

Daily writing is a type of training ground where you act as your own coach, firm but gentle, rigorous but compassionate. Only you can tell how much and how often is best for you to write. Most of us need to experiment a little and to remember that over time our writing needs change. This month you may find yourself deeply involved in a chapter of your novel, writing a few hours over the weekend and one evening a week. But next month, as you feel yourself losing touch with the plot, you may need to put the novel aside and spend a week or two writing a page a day in your journal about the main characters.

There are two ways to structure daily writing to percolate: You can decide on a set amount of time each day to sit and write. Some people schedule a regular time, while others do their daily writing as the spirit moves them. An alternative approach is to decide on a certain number of pages and to write regardless of the amount of time it takes you to complete them. I suggest you give both methods a try to see which you feel more comfortable with. Next, decide the period of time you'd like to experiment with daily writing. Three weeks? Two months? One year? Finally, decide what you will write.

1. Will you free-write each day, letting whatever idea strikes you be your subject?
2. Will you work on a particular piece or body of work?
3. Will you choose a single subject to explore?

When you make decisions about quantity, be reasonable. Even if you wish you could write ten pages or for six hours, if your desire doesn't fit easily into your life, don't set yourself up to fail. Pick a length of time or a number of pages to write that's comfortable and realistic. The same goes for the duration of your daily writing practice. For instance, maybe you have a week's vacation and you can write five pages a day for seven days. Perhaps it's soccer season and you have half an hour to write between carpools until ice hockey gets under way. Three words or three pages, for two months or four days, for thirty minutes or four hours, begin where you can succeed.

As a tribute to honor the death of his friend, poet William Stafford, Robert Bly wrote a poem every single day for one full year before he left his bed in the morning. From his daily practice evolved the wonderful book *Morning Poems,* which contains 82 poems culled from the 365. You don't have to copy what Bly did—though it's hard to resist—but once you establish your daily writing practice, you must follow through with it by sitting down and simply beginning to write. You can use a bound journal, a computer file, or loose paper. If you've chosen to free-write, then begin with a random word or phrase from the dictionary, a book of writing prompts, or the first idea that pops into your head, and go from there in any direction your thoughts take you. If you've chosen a particular project to work on, then for whatever length of time you've committed to, sit down and add to what you've already written about it. If you choose to explore a single topic, then begin each session by writing the topic on the top of your page and write down whatever thoughts and ideas that come to you, even if they don't, at first, appear to be related to your topic. Whichever plan you choose, don't become rigid about it. Trust your Writing Self and your intuition. If you're free-writing and no matter what word or phrase you start with, you find yourself returning to a single topic, revise your plan and concentrate on the topic at hand.

The first time I tried daily writing, in my twenties, it wasn't my idea. I was visiting an ashram regularly, trying to get grounded. I found meditation exasperating. My mind would race on and on, and I felt like a failure. At the end of one evening meditation when it was my turn for the Guru to tap my head with a wand of peacock feathers, I blurted out something about how confused I felt. A few moments later a woman told me that the Guru wanted her to help me. I mentioned my struggle with writing, and she recommended that I go home and write every day for three hours, for three months.

I was intrigued and nervous. It took me several weeks to structure my schedule in a way that made three-hour writing sessions possible. But I was single, without children, and teaching part-time at a couple of colleges. So I was able to arrange one semester around writing instead of the other way around. Right away, I decided that the woman had meant every *week*day. I took the weekends off. At first, I couldn't let the phone ring unanswered. After all, the schedule she recommended didn't specify three *uninterrupted* hours of writing. So I'd sit down at my basement desk every morning at nine and not emerge until twelve, eventually ignoring the phone. Even in my imperfect way, I was committed.

The pieces I wrote during that three-month period were the most ambitious I'd yet attempted. I broke through blocks I didn't know I had. I gave my Writing Self time, space, and energy to evolve. I surprised myself. Then, once the three months were over, I abandoned the practice for about four years. But the practice didn't abandon me.

The breakthroughs I'd made didn't dissolve over time. In fact, over time my periodic forays with daily writing to percolate not only energized my Writing Self, they taught me the discipline and focus necessary for completing books. By the time the proposal for *Room to Write* was accepted, I knew how to use daily writing to help me complete it.

Through my experience with writing daily I also discovered that as a writer I'm both a Stickler and a Rebel. I'm driven to complete what I've committed to write, yet I fight against the rigidity of a set goal. Once I realized I had these opposing impulses, I learned ways to balance them when I write. For instance, when I wrote *Room to Write,* I took out a calendar and, counting backward from the manuscript's due date, gave myself the goal of twenty-five pages a week, or five pages a day for five days with two days off. Now I had a schedule that would satisfy the Stickler in me as long as I got my twenty-five pages done before each Sunday night. The Rebel in me was also appeased because I had the leeway of choosing which two days not to write and of writing more than five pages on the days when I was on a roll. Through daily writing I refined my understanding of my Writing Self so that I could tailor my writing schedule to be successful.

Discipline, Not Torture

I admit that during my first daily writing sessions I took liberties with my interpretation of what "daily" meant. Even today, as I write the first draft of this book, I get up periodically, make a cup of tea, check e-mail, do one or two small chores like mixing up marinade for tonight's fish supper. Sometimes it feels like I'm cheating my Writing Self of time, or my readers of my full attention to this book, or my family of the money we're spending on child care so I can write. But in truth, even during daily writing sessions, I need these small interludes to break away, stretch a bit. During long writing sessions, pausing periodically allows the next wave of creation to form. The pauses are mini percolation periods. As long as I'm not using them to break the spell or to interrupt the flow of my writing, five minutes to pair socks gives an idea a chance to briefly swirl freely again before I get back to capturing it in words. After all, haven't we all had at least one great idea in the bathroom?

Practice

∼ DELVING INTO DAILY WRITING

The part of the percolation process that daily writing energizes depends on how you do it. Here are four techniques to exercise different ways of percolating out loud:

1. *To become conscious of percolation.* For a week, allot yourself a much shorter time than you actually have available for daily writing. If you have thirty minutes, give yourself only ten minutes and then stop writing no matter what. As an alternative, you can try limiting the number of pages/lines/paragraphs/words you write. If you usually write three pages, write only one page. With the rest of the time, pay attention to your thoughts, especially how they relate to what you were just writing about. In this way you intensify and become more conscious of the way you percolate, and you give it extra time. This technique is similar to eating one cookie instead of several. It helps you savor the experience of percolation the way eating a single cookie makes you appreciate the full flavor instead of dulling it by eating cookies until you aren't truly tasting them anymore.

2. *To think in writing.* For a week, stretch your daily writing practice beyond its current limit. If you usually write for thirty minutes, write for forty. The extra writing time will coax you to think in writing. During the extra ten minutes, write without stopping to think about

what you're going to say, without crossing out, without rereading what comes before, without needing to be neat, and without even needing what you write to make sense. Midweek it should become a bit less awkward to write and think at once. By the week's end, you will be familiar with it and, with continued practice, on your way to becoming a fluent thinker in writing.

3. *To deepen your percolative faculties.* Choose one subject and write about it for your usual amount of time but return to the subject every day for three full weeks. Coming back to the same topic day after day will challenge you to make deeper, wilder connections to it and see new angles of your subject out of sheer necessity to keep writing about the topic. This technique exercises the faculties that you use naturally as you percolate. As a result, you'll strengthen your percolation abilities. But don't overdo it. Use this practice only occasionally so as not to put undue stress on your Writing Self, which causes your ability to free-associate to shut down in protest rather than to thrive.

4. *To broaden your percolative faculties.* If you already have the kind of temperament that compels you to contemplate an idea for a long time, you might *broaden* your percolation faculties through three weeks of daily writing purposely with no particular subject in mind. Each day begin with a random thought or phrase that has nothing to do with the project you're working on. You're in the midst of writing a screenplay about democracy, and as you get ready to write you make a mental note that the laundry is piling up; start your writing with the laundry that day. The point of this practice is to widen your breadth of perception. The way you ordinarily contemplate democracy in a daily writing practice might be to explore all the ramifications of it in a person's life. Your thought line takes you deeper, in a vertical direction. But when you begin your daily writing with an unrelated topic such as doing your laundry, eventually you begin to see surprising connections in the form of metaphors and analogies between democracy and some of the random writing topics. Now your percolation process is also moving in a wider, more horizontal way.

When I do this practice I collect random thoughts to use ahead of time. That way, I don't get stuck in the trap of not having a random thought when I'm ready to write. On a notepad, I keep a small collection of intriguing phrases I hear or see, such as the title of a display I noticed at the grocery store: Now That You're Out of Prison, What's Next?

subject: the critters #1
in back of book

Seven

SO, DID YOU
WRITE TODAY?

I have a colleague who tortured himself while he wrote his first novel. He's an award-winning fiction writer and a terrific story-teller. But because he had placed impossibly high expectations on himself and his novel, he found the writing process so painful that he'd often be unable to get the next section or scene down on his computer. Completing his novel became more of a nightmare than a thrilling challenge. He frequently came over to my house around dinnertime, close to tears. Our conversation would go something like this:

"I couldn't write today." His voice was full of shame and disgust, as though he were confessing to mugging a nun.

"Wait a minute," I'd say. "Nothing? Not a single word?"

"Zippo. I'm still on page eighty-seven."

"So what have you been doing the last six hours?"

He'd answer with one or more of the following:

"Staring at a blank screen between starting sentences and delet-ing them/Rereading the last twenty pages and realizing they're crap/ Journaling about what a lousy father I'd be since I can't take care of my main character for even a hundred pages/Reading the newspaper looking for a better plot line than mine/Rereading *Anna Karenina* to remind myself how a *real* novelist does it."

"So you wrote today," I'd say.

"Are you hard of hearing?" he'd bark.

Over dinner, we'd discuss where he was in the manuscript. Usually, he'd borrow some paper to make a few notes and, I suspect, go home and write into the night.

He's a perfect example of someone losing touch with the subtler processes of writing, such as percolation. As with my colleague's case, being out of touch with percolation can skew our thinking and narrow our understanding of what writing means. We become critical of our Writing Self and we start to keep a mental scorecard: The days we write go on the winning side and the days we don't make us losers. Writing becomes a proving ground rather than a source of nourishment.

People tell me that they want help to write more. They haven't written in months, they tell me, or it takes them ages to finish anything. They can write only once a week/when in crisis/in a journal/poetry (or some other genre). Because their underlying struggle is so often about accepting the whole of what it means to write, before suggesting ways they can shift their writing tendencies, I ask people to explore three questions.

1. Do you accept and embrace your desire to write?
2. Can you accept who you are?
3. Will you trust that the aspects of your personality that you need to write develop through the act of writing?

It may at first sound ridiculous to ask people who are taking a writing workshop and who also may be extremely distraught about their writing life if they've accepted their desire to write. Isn't it obvious they're already investing their time, money, and energy into writing? But actually, we're all capable of acting on enormous desires that we have not fully accepted or embraced. If you decide you want to write a novel but your ideas keep coming out in essay form, do you feel grateful that your genre has appeared so emphatically, or excited to meet the possible challenge of learning how to integrate novel writing with essay writing? Or are you frustrated because you're not meeting the goal you've set for yourself?

Accept and Embrace Your Desire

When you recognize at what level you accept your desire to write, you can free yourself to write more and to delight in how the different stages of writing interact, interweave, and inspire one another. The fact is, you can't always control how much and about what you write. What you *can* do is commit to the work of writing, which includes accepting the time involved in the process and whatever result emerges at the end. To embrace your desire to write often means letting go of the idealized images or fantasies you have about it.

Someone once explained to me that the difference between prayer and meditation is that prayer is talking to one's God and meditation is listening. My writer colleague mistrusted the listening. He felt secure that his novel was progressing only when he was in dialogue with it. His ability to pray, in the writerly sense, seemed more essential to him than his ability to meditate. We all have a tendency to impose value judgments on the various work we do, often based on how well we feel we do it. You may consider cleaning the house less important than cooking a good meal, or being on time less important than looking your best. My colleague—and many, many writers—considers percolating to be less important than the process of physically getting the words down. With this attitude, they are embracing only part of what it means to write.

The best way I know to first accept and then improve your relationship to writing is to begin by facing any preconceived notions you may have about what it means to write. I started my own self-examination by acknowledging the ways I subconsciously rank the work of writing. Here is what I found my hierarchy to be:

Creating new material
↓
Writing in my journal
↓
Revising new material
↓
Editing revised material

I was holding the belief that creating new material was much more important than editing and improving existing material. Like my novelist friend, I used to feel productive, engaged in "real" writing, only when I was in the process of generating brand-new material. Journal writing was okay but really only second best, and revising and editing were something I did grudgingly or not at all. Missing altogether from my hierarchy was percolation, the time spent doing research for a piece, and organizing my drafts and notes as I wrote.

Once I recognized my preconceived ideas, the next step was to figure out where they came from so I could evaluate their validity. My undergraduate and graduate studies, I realized, had emphasized recognizing and mastering various elements of writing, such as establishing voice, sustaining tension, and using metaphor. My teachers rarely talked about the writing process except to define its stages: brainstorming, first draft, revision, editing, final copy. This was the progression from which I developed my hierarchy.

Looking back, I realized I didn't ask about process or even pay much attention to it. I think I was scared I might not be a real writer, and I wanted at least to keep up appearances by learning the universally accepted stages necessary for good writing. I assumed if I followed them in order, one would prepare the way for the next.

I was wrong. After school, the hierarchy I'd internalized became something I tried to fit the facets of writing into. As long as I stayed attached to that order, I struggled through many pieces and abandoned many more. I tired easily, questioned my abilities, and enjoyed only a small portion of the process of writing.

I left school believing that process was like a secret handshake that, once discovered, would gain my writing the approving nods of my elders. From family, other writers, and the media I picked up more ideas about how writing is supposed to progress. I absorbed the perspective that writers struggle, that talent is paramount, that success is luck. Once I looked closely at my preconceived beliefs about writing, I realized that in order to truly embrace my desire to write, I had to give up these views or else remain frustrated and eventually even turn bitter.

It would have been nearly impossible to give up my views without replacing them with new ones. Fortunately, as a writing teacher I'd already learned to readjust my expectations about writing when I taught my first college composition class to a group of juniors and seniors who'd never been asked to organize their writing before. Dismayed, I turned to another teacher I respected, and she gave me sage advice: Pick one aspect of writing that you can feel successful teaching and they can feel successful learning. I tossed away my syllabus and some of my previous expectations along with it, and my students ended up becoming better writers.

So I knew that I could find alternative ways of looking at writing from other writers and teachers I trusted. I also began to read books with many points of view about the writing process. This was enormously helpful in putting my old views to rest because I now saw them as part of a spectrum. I began to approach writing the way I choreographed a dance piece, intuitively and experimentally. By borrowing approaches from dance, a creative process in which I already felt satisfied, I came to truly understand the adage, You already know what you need.

Accept Who You Are

I've described my experience as an example of how, as you clear away your own detrimental notions and find sources for better alternatives, you can come to fully accept your desire to write. The next step is to accept the person who is writing, meaning your personal circumstance, rhythm, and nature. Your personality has a direct bearing on your Writing Self.

"How much do you write?" I'm often asked. Most people really want to know if there's a magic number of pages or hours that makes one a legitimate writer. My answer always surprises me. When not working on a specific project with a deadline, my general habit was to write for two to three hours a day, five days a week. When I think about this, it's amazing to me that I organized my entire life to support two-ish hours a day of work. On the surface it doesn't seem to add up to much of a day. But I'd spend those writing hours creating new work, revising it, and editing it. I'd spend the balance of my working-writer day reading and researching, teaching, and doing the ever-expanding tasks of the business side of my profession: correspondence, follow-up, filling out grant applications, working on book proposals, making and returning telephone calls, and brainstorming about other avenues for sharing my work to pay the rent.

It's a small amount of time, those two to three hours daily. Couldn't I make it longer if I didn't socialize, take yoga classes, make art, read, see movies, spend time with my family, help the occasional stranger, and comfort troubled friends? I don't believe so because my sense of self includes all of the above just as much as writing. I'm also not convinced I would get more writing accomplished if I gave up some of these other activities because I don't have the wherewithal, even if I had the time, to write more. After a few hours, I'm spent.

I'm impressed by writers who also have full-time jobs. One of my college classmates is a full-time lawyer who has published two short-story collections and a novel. He wrote them during his daily one-hour train commute between Baltimore and Washington, D.C. I am not this type of person. When I'm working on a specific project, I need to give over whole days to writing a first draft. Even if I physically write for only a few of those hours, I need to immerse myself, without distraction, in my subject for the day.

My rhythm used to make me feel like a dilettante and a fake, or worse, a mediocre writer. I envied my colleagues who had the security of a comfortable salary, the energy for another way to contribute to society, the focus, and the comfort of fitting into the societal norm. But I had to accept *my* reality:

1. I was not like them.
2. Spending energy being bitter about this takes away from writing time.
3. I'm already committed to being a writer no matter what.

There's no guarantee that having a Writing Self is easy, but perhaps we focus too much attention on how hard it can be given our personal circumstances or rhythm. Instead of judging yourself so harshly, if you accept who you are you can enjoy the writing process as *you* experience it. Whether it's life circumstances or personality traits that define how you write, you may be better off working within their confines instead of expending potential writing energy being aggravated by them. Author Peter Korn's writing time is defined by being a father. Because he shares work and parenting responsibilities with his wife, his writing schedule changes all year long in conjunction with his children's school calendar. As a result, he does a lot of magazine work these days because it lends itself to his time frame. Meanwhile, his next novel percolates away in the back of his mind until the kids are old enough to go to sleep-away camp. I remember hearing a true story about the writer who would get up in the morning and have his wife lock him in his office. At noon she would unlock the door, serve him lunch, and ask, "How did the writing go this morning?" "Wonderfully," he'd reply. "I put a comma in." His wife would lock the writer back in his office until dinner, when she would ask him how the writing went during the afternoon. "Splendidly," he'd answer. "I took the comma out."

What You Need Develops as You Write

Psychologist Anthony Storr has found that people drawn to writing tend toward complexity, incompleteness, individuality, impulsiveness, and expansiveness. There are other studies that claim writers are more prone to mental illness than are other groups of people because we, as a group, have a lesser capacity to filter our environment and are therefore easily overwhelmed or confused by it. Whether or not we recognize ourselves in these characteristics, each of us has personality traits that affect our Writing Self. Because of my natural tendencies, I, for example, am not made up of the characteristics that most support novel writing. I tend not to have the talent of keeping several story lines going at once that helps in the writing of a full-length piece of fiction. That doesn't mean I can't write a novel, but it does mean that when I decide to work in that genre, I am doing *two* things: writing a novel and cultivating traits that aren't intrinsically a part of who I am.

The good news is that just as our personality affects our writing, our writing affects our personal makeup. Through my writing I've nurtured playfulness, courage, humor, faith, discipline, balance, and accountability. I would never have had the nerve to parent if I hadn't first extended these qualities through my Writing Self. Just as with parenting, I develop more of what I need to write with integrity as I go along. My understanding of what it means to parent or to write grows with time and experience. There's no way to know that the traits you need to evolve as a writer will develop along with your writing, except by experiencing it firsthand. You have to take the time to reflect on the changes in your writing style or habits in order to notice the shifts.

Once you accept the scope of what's involved in writing and your own strengths and challenges as a writer, it becomes more obvious how you've already grown in your writing. It is at this point that you can replace the fearful, self-critical voice that asks, Did you write today? with the legitimate question, What did you do for your Writing Self today? The new question makes room for you to accept that when it comes to writing, everything counts. Even what you throw away. My troubled novelist friend thought that if he deleted everything he wrote, he hadn't written anything. But he *had* written; he simply hadn't kept what he wrote that day.

It's almost absurd to question whether you wrote on any given day. It's like asking, Did you practice yoga today? Would the answer be no if you didn't attend a class or do a series of poses at home? Yoga is much more than putting one's body in certain positions. In fact, the practice of the poses is meant to support a way of being in the world on a daily, moment-to-moment basis. So if on any given day you use your breath to focus or concentrate, or you adjust your posture to help shift your attitude, or you use a single aspect of one pose in order to stretch and refresh yourself, then you practiced yoga.

In the same way, it's fair to say that you wrote today if you spent ten minutes rereading the last three pages of your short story and you made a note to switch two paragraphs or nix the description of the bicycle. You wrote today if you heard a news story that gave you an idea for a poem. You wrote today if you looked up a fact or two about hernias on the Internet as research for a character in your novel. When your Writing Self is engaged and aligned, you'll find that there are daily occurrences in your life that relate to and feed whatever writing project you're working on. You'll be attuned, attentive, receptive. You won't be able to go through a day *without* writing.

Practice

∾ ACCEPT, EMBRACE, DEVELOP

Remember the biblical maxim "Physician, heal thyself"? I say to you, Writer, know thyself! This set of practices will help you to gain acceptance of your Writing Self. Once you have acknowledged your traits as a writer, you will be able to work with them to meet your writing goals.

1. *Accept*: Write down your own writing process hierarchy. First, make a list of all the phases and elements of the writing process from percolation to making it public. Don't leave out anything, not even organizing your notes and your writing desk. Next, rank each element in order of your priorities. In other words, even if intellectually you know that revising is just as important as creating new material, if when you write, you dread the former and feel excited by the latter, then you'd rank creating material above rewriting it. It's very important to be honest about your feelings and your relationship to each element of writing. Once you've completed the ranking, rewrite your list in a diagram similar to mine on page 57.

Give yourself some time—between twenty minutes and a few days—to contemplate your hierarchy. Then set aside an hour to write in your journal about where your rankings came from. As you examine and explore your best guesses at the sources of your beliefs, try not to judge yourself. Before you can shift out of a belief that isn't serving you, such as Publishing is the most important reason to write, you'll want to affirm a new belief to replace it with, such as Each phase of writing supports my satisfaction as a writer. Look for your new beliefs in this book, from your other creative outlets, and from fellow writers and artists who enjoy what they do. To remind yourself of a new way of thinking, post it on your writing desk.

2. *Embrace*: This two-phase exercise will make you more aware of

your writing rhythm. In phase one, set aside three days when you can write, uninterrupted, for as long as you like. The days don't have to be consecutive. Each day, write down your starting time. As you write, pay attention to how you feel. When your mind gets fuzzy or a part of your body bothers you, like your eyes get tired or you can't stop yawning or negative self-talk makes it hard to concentrate, note the time and take a break that adds up to ten minutes for every hour you've been writing. A half hour after your break is done, note whether you're feeling more energized or clearheaded. If not, stop writing and note the time again. If you are feeling revived, keep writing and repeating this process until your session becomes a struggle. Chart the times you've noted each day to get an idea of how long a productive writing session is for you. Whether it's two hours or ten hours, this is your natural rhythm. People who can write for several hours at once don't always have the time to devote to such long stretches. This can be one of the sources of their frustration as a writer. If you're one of these writers, make sure to carve out at least one weekly or monthly session in which you can write into the night. Knowing that there will be a time and place for you to write in your natural rhythm often alleviates a layer of your dissatisfaction.

For the second phase of this exercise, review the writing you've done over the past year. Add up the number of pieces you've written by genre to determine the modes you are most comfortable writing in. If you've written ten poems, one novel, and three essays, it reflects that you probably use different writing genres to balance one another. In the midst of a long work, writing something brief and more associative, such as a poem, nurtures aspects of the Writing Self that a novel doesn't. But if the inventory of your writing is more like one novel and three short stories, or twelve poems, thirty journal entries, and two children's picture books, you may discern a noticeable pattern in the type of writing that best suits your personality. The first list shows someone who is drawn to narrative. The second list suggests a writer who likes to work in short forms. Again, you can cultivate any genre you want, but by being aware of your natural tendencies, you'll approach a genre knowing beforehand if you'll be cultivating it as well as creating a piece of writing. By anticipating what you're undertaking, you can go into it with a mind-set that will most support your Writing Self. So if you've been writing one-page journal entries for the past year and you decide to write a novel, you won't expect your Writing Self to produce a twenty-page chapter right off the bat.

3. *Develop*: To nudge the cynical part of your mind to admit, however grudgingly, that indeed you can develop the writing skills you need through writing, list on a piece of paper three aspects of your Writing Self you love and three aspects you consider to be challenges. Notice if any of the strengths are the flip side of any of the challenges. For instance, a strength might be that you take risks by writing in various genres. A challenge might involve taking risks in subject matter. If you find no apparent correlation between your strengths and challenges, write down one former writing challenge that has lessened for you and a brief account of how this came to be. One of my challenges was following through on an idea for a book-length project. I was accustomed to writing poems and short essays. So I used a weekly writing support group as a place to commit to each phase of turning a concept into a book proposal until I'd followed through on the initial idea. Through my experience I learned how to chunk down a big idea or project into smaller, manageable bits that I could think of as poems and essays. By first accepting my current limitations, I was able to use them to help me fulfill a writing desire.

Body - Mind Exercise

❧ ACCEPT YOURSELF

To become more aware of the level at which you accept your own desire to write, do the following exercise: Sitting or standing, stretch your arms over your head and say aloud or silently, "I accept my desire to write." Now stretch your arms out to the sides and say it again. Next, reach or clasp your hands behind your back so that your chest opens a little and say it again. Finally, wrap your arms around your chest as if you were hugging yourself, your hands resting somewhere in your shoulder/shoulder blade area, and say it. Now rewrap your arms around your chest with the opposite arm on top and say it again. Notice if there are any positions that feel more uncomfortable than others—not just physically but psychically. Signs of this include welling with emotion, flashing on an image or memory, feeling spacey, your voice faltering. The positions you find more difficult correspond to the aspects of your Writing Self that need new tools to help them to thrive. I suggest the following interpretation of what each position represents in terms of aspects of writing:

arms above the head = the spiritual aspect
arms out to the side = the communal aspect
arms clasped behind the back = being open to risk or vulnerability
hugging left arm below, right arm above = self-protection
hugging left arm above, right arm below = self-acceptance

Whichever aspect of your Writing Self you're uncomfortable with relates to where you may lack acceptance of your Writing Self. If your sore spot is the communal, work on shifting your attitude about the relationship between your writing and its place in the world. If your sore place is self-protection, look more closely at how protecting yourself may interfere with what you want to write about or how you want to write it. If all the postures felt hard, or you aren't sure how they felt, as a point of comparison, try the exact same series of arm positions, only this time say, "I accept my desire to_____," filling in the blank with a desire you've already accepted and are practicing, such as the desire to swim regularly or to practice meditation or to laugh more.

Eight

PERCOLATION OBSTACLES

Writer's block is a constellation of obstacles not just to writing but also to feeling satisfied as a writer. When you experience an obstacle it's because your Writing Self has been compromised. This is similar to the way the physical body gets aggravated by an infection or a virus. In the written world someone else's obstacle doesn't infect you like a physical virus. But blockages are just as threatening as physical diseases, in that blockages sap you of your mental and emotional vitality and turn writing into a chore, a miserable marriage between you and your words, a cross to bear. If your obstacles are short-lived, like common colds, they will dissipate on their own over time. But if you experience any blockage as chronic, recurring, or debilitating, you must treat it. Whether cyclic or ongoing, your obstacles are probably caused by neglecting an aspect of the percolation process if you experience them in one of these ways:

1. If you feel like you don't have time to write
2. If you believe that you don't have anything to say
3. If you are paralyzed by critical thoughts about your writing

Let's consider these issues individually.

Breaking the Time Barrier

If your obstacle to writing is that the rest of your life is too busy and demanding, I'll tell you a secret: *There's no such thing as not having any time to write.* There's only not having *enough* time. Even the people who make their living writing and so devote their whole work week to it still sometimes feel they need more time.

Fortunately, time isn't as fixed as we pretend it is. For instance, you've probably experienced minutes that seem like hours when you are doing work you dislike, and you've experienced days that seem like minutes while doing what you love. When you don't write and you believe it's because you have no time, you're limiting your idea of what writing actually means. Remember, everything counts in the written world. So if you don't have time to write a poem, you *do* have time to jot down a line or a thought. And when you don't have time to write a short story, you have time to think about the story's main character while you're on hold on the phone or standing in line at the deli counter. You can examine your fingernails, the person in line in front of you, and you can percolate, percolate. By doing this you're engaging your Writing Self, respecting its presence, its hunger; you're cultivating your time, which makes your sense of time more flexible and fluid. One of two things occurs as a result. A day of writing time becomes available that wasn't before, or because of the percolation time you've invested in the midst of the rest of your life, you accomplish in an hour of writing what might have taken many hours. Either way, eventually you will find that an hour will open up into a day's worth of writing.

"But that's not how I work," you say.

How do you know until you've made the time to give it a try?

Overcoming Nothing to Say

Both seasoned and new writers hit the wall of feeling they have nothing to say. It happens when the Writing Self is depleted, often after completing a writing project. The last chapter takes everything out of you; you feel spent; you have absolutely nothing else to say about your subject or anything else; every thought in your head is a dull, greeting-card sentiment.

Before you put words down again you may need time and space to replenish yourself. Experiment. Take three days away from creating new writing and use it to read, spend the day listening to music (it's okay to dance to it), cook, lie belly-down to smell and touch the earth/concrete/linoleum with your hands and cheeks.

If that doesn't work, you're probably placing unreasonable demands on your Writing Self, and it's shutting down in protest. Check your expectations. You might have nothing to say because you haven't given yourself enough percolation time. Or you might be thinking thoughts such as, "This better be good" or, "I already know it's going to bomb." Both statements and others similar to them voice a lack of faith in your Writing Self. So does, "If I don't pound out three pages this session I might as well forget writing." Focus instead on clarifying the reasons you want to write right now. Your reasons could include discovery, clarity, catharsis, recognition, obligation, protest, pleasure. Once you reestablish your purpose, write it down at the top of the page you're trying to begin. Do this every time you sit down to write for a while to help remind you that you *do* have something to say because you have a reason to say it. This practice will also get you in the habit of percolating before each writing session.

If your reason for writing hasn't crystallized, then try to percolate out loud to discover it. Just start writing and see what develops. You could even begin your writing sessions a few times by writing the phrase "The reason I want to write is . . ." and go from there. Don't worry if you can't stick with one reason. It's common for the reason for writing a piece to change as you go. The thrust past this obstacle is devoting some percolation time to why you are writing. It takes the pressure off you to produce and reconnects you to your sense of purpose.

Deflating Self-Criticism

Self-criticism flares up during writing, rewriting, and going public as well, but it's most cunning when it appears during the percolation phase. In the rest of the writing process you make decisions based on your judgments. In a first draft, for example, you choose to write down *these* words instead of *those* words. Then rewriting is all about looking again at what you already have. Finally, when you share your work, you reshape it either vocally, as you present it, or physically, if it's in print form. So within these stages of writing it's easy for your capacity to evaluate your work to turn into disparaging it.

But during percolation there are no written words to act on yet, just ideas and images floating around in your psyche and courting your Writing Self. There's no reason to engage in your opinions. If you neglect percolation, you give up its time to your critical facilities. As a result you begin to form more opinions than images and ideas. Because both your images and ideas and your critical opinions reside in your psyche, they're like two cats eating from the same food dish. The more aggressive cat will usually push the other aside and eat all the food.

The inner critical voice tends to be stronger than the voice within saying, "I have an idea!" When you repeatedly give up your percolation process, self-criticism co-opts it, and you develop an overblown critical voice and a starved intuitive, creative voice. When I picture my Writing Self overwhelmed by self-criticism, the critical half is a huge zeppelin crushing the intuitive half, which is shrunken like a dried-up turnip. Most of us are already experts at judging and criticizing ourselves in other areas of our lives. So when we engage our Writing Self it's no surprise that it's easy for us to forgo percolation and cripple our writing ideas with critical thoughts.

Practice

The exercises that follow specifically address writing obstacles related to the percolation process. Use these suggestions when you are in the midst of these barriers to help you get past them, or better yet, as preventative medicine if you think you're prone to any of them.

∾ BREAKING THE "I HAVE NO TIME" BARRIER

The way to overcome the belief that you have no time is to develop a keener awareness of how time is related to your writing. The following practices challenge your sense of writing time.

Regardless of how much time you have to devote to writing, every day for two weeks do something for your writing for only five minutes. Even if you find yourself with an unexpected free hour, don't use it to write. Any and all writing you do during the two weeks can take place for only five minutes a day. Limiting your writing time to such a short period may frustrate you, but that frustration should make it glaringly obvious all the other times that you could be writing. You may also be surprised at just how much you can accomplish in five minutes a day. Conscious of the time limit, your Writing Self may intensify its percolation activity so that when you do sit to write, your ideas flow. Often the sense that we have no time to write is a misperception, and this exercise can provide you with insight into whether or not that's true for you. One person I know completed an outline of a novel during this two-week practice.

A second practice to try for two weeks is keeping a daily record of what you do for your Writing Self. Your goal is to notice something you did each day. Whether you've read a few pages of this book, written in your journal, organized your writing desk, reread something you've written, noted an enticing fact you might like to write about, rethought something about the main character of your story, attended a reading at a place you'd like to read someday, finished writing a chapter, percolated, or fiddled with some of the magnetic words on your refrigerator, they all count as actions that are nourishing for your Writing Self. Even if you do only one thing a day for your writing, over the weeks, months, and years, those things add up.

The point of this practice is to become aware of all that you already do to support your writing. Some people might argue that several of the activities I list sound like ways to avoid writing, ways to procrastinate, but I would disagree. It's just that attitude, that the only real act of writing is putting words down, that can damage your connection to the writing process and cause such obstacles as the mistaken belief that you have no time to write.

∼ OVERCOMING NOTHING TO SAY

Sometimes feeling like you have nothing to say is, at its core, a fear or belief that you don't have anything interesting or new to say. To find out if this is at the root of your block, read over ten pages of your writer's journal and pick one idea or thought from those pages. On a new page, start writing about that idea again. Don't summarize what you've already written. Instead, write about your idea in a different genre (such as poetry or a letter), or write about the idea humorously instead of seriously, or vice versa. If you don't keep a writer's journal, then choose an idea another writer has written about and write about it yourself in your own way. Most writers use their writing to say what they have to say many times over but from different angles. The common wisdom is that there really isn't anything new for us to say anyway. Rather, as writers our role is to tell the same stories and pose the same questions and answers that humankind has been considering throughout history, but to do so from the perspective of our unique makeup and our particular place in time. From this viewpoint you're relieved of the pressure of writing something unique. So retell a favorite tale or myth, one that captivates you. Put in all the details that you have used to embellish the story in your mind, the ones that have been percolating since you first heard or read the story—Robin Hood's childhood, Sleeping Beauty's dreams, Noah's journal from his forty days on the ark.

Another reason for feeling like you have nothing to say comes from losing touch with your intention when writing. Intention is your purpose for writing that day: catharsis, understanding, pleasure, discovery, obligation (as in a deadline you must meet), protest, clarity. My intention today is to gather and clarify my thoughts. Knowing that, I have a starting point. I approach my writing with a reason. I gather up my thoughts into sentences and then work to make them as clear as possible. If my intention was discovery, I'd write solely for the purpose of finding out what I had to say on a particular subject today or in general. Being connected to a specific reason to write can generate as much writing as having a topic to write about.

For your next five writing sessions, start by writing down a one- or two-word intention at the top of your page. As you write, keep your intention firmly in mind. If you start to feel blocked or lost, reread your intention. If you don't know your intention, then pick one that appeals to you and use it for this writing practice. You can even choose five intentions ahead of time and try out one each day that you do this practice. One of the best pieces of advice I've ever received was, At the brick wall, turn left. All of these exercises will help you to overcome having nothing to say in the same spirit—without really having to think of anything to say.

∾ BUSTING THE SELF-CRITIC

This is one of the most challenging practices I offer. Not everyone has the nerve to do it, but even just thinking about doing it can help some people deflate the self-critic that berates their Writing Self and saps their creative energy. At its essence, this practice is about exposing the tormenting critic, taking the sting out of its bite, shining the light on the dark beast so it can be seen for what it truly is: incessant, arbitrary chatter.

For your next four writing sessions delete or throw away everything you write. Pay attention to what your critical voice says each time you toss your writing. Does it condemn you for destroying gems as loudly as it maligned what you were writing prior to this exercise? If so, let this be proof that the self-critical voice is simply that—a voice that pipes up with reproach indiscriminately. If you write diligently it will condemn what you've written, but as soon as you concede to the voice's negative judgments, without skipping a beat it will admonish you for throwing away your best work. The reason this happens is that the self-critical voice is one-dimensional. It simply attacks whatever is in front of it. It's like a tumbleweed of all the negative messages we've been exposed to that blows around in our consciousness. Once you recognize how arbitrary it is, it loses a lot of its power to harm you.

A second benefit of this exercise is how it strengthens your percolation powers as you notice which passages you wrote and tossed stick with your Writing Self, percolating away in spite of the lack of written words.

Body-Mind Exercise

∼ LOOSEN YOUR GRIP

Try this simple yoga technique when you have an idea you want to write about and you feel blocked. Gently place the tip of your tongue between the back of your two front teeth and take deep breaths. Breathing with the tongue in this position relaxes the jaw, which in turn helps to relax your whole face, neck, and shoulder area. Take at least two releasing breaths with attention to your jaw, face, neck, and shoulders, respectively. Now, with your tongue still in its pose, take five deep breaths as you focus your attention on your writing idea. If you feel yourself tense up or your mind become critical of your idea, go back to using your breath to relax your jaw, face, neck, and shoulders. The relaxation effect of this exercise on your body helps you to relax about your idea, which gives it more room to develop. Go back to giving five breaths to your writing idea. When you've completed your five breaths, start writing. Use the tongue-pose exercise often, and eventually just placing your tongue in the pose will remind you to loosen up your expectations of yourself as you write.

II
REVISION

We must learn to see the world anew.

EINSTEIN

Nine

LOOK AGAIN (AND AGAIN . . .): REVISION

O ften people consider revision to be drudge work or simply baffling. It's at the top of most of the informal "what I like least about writing" surveys that I conduct during workshops. But I consider revising an aspect of human nature, a natural process. We do it in our minds as we write a letter, on the computer screen when we e-mail, and out loud when we rehearse what we want to say to someone. We even revise our language in the midst of a conversation based on the responses we're getting.

Revising or rewriting encompasses all the ways you work on an idea from the first draft until the time you decide the piece is finished. There are many methods of revising. Any of them will nurture your Writing Self once you understand why rewriting is nourishing.

In a sense, our very physical development as infants is a process of revision. Watch a baby. First she learns to crawl. For a while, that's a good enough way to get around. Then her mastery spurs her on to walk, run, run faster, climb, and jump. The drive to evolve, to take the next step, to build on and deepen what we already know, is innate.

We bring this built-in push with us into the activities of adulthood. Revising is the Writing Self's version of this urge.

Sometimes in our writing life, this spirit of discovery that revision is all about gets dislocated. Maybe for you, it's been repressed, stunted, or overly developed. If so, you probably approach revision with your critical faculties leading the way. You look at a piece to see what's wrong with it, rather than looking with your creative intuition guiding you to help your piece evolve. I often imagine the Critic and the Creator as twins: god and goddess of the psyche. At first glance, the two look alike and we confuse which is in the lead. When it comes to revision, we need both of them, but it must be intuition, rather than criticism, that guides the way for rewriting to filter through the desire to grow and progress that's instinctive from birth. As you prepare to revise, steeling yourself to be uncompromisingly picky about every word in your draft puts your critic in charge. But starting to revise with curiosity and anticipation about how the draft will develop is inviting intuition as your guide.

Another tendency common to people who have issues with rewriting is that they are Functionally Fixed, a term developed by writer and educator Ben Reynolds. This refers to the ways in which we routinely do things because they work for us. For instance, every morning I shower first thing. It helps me wake up gently, and it gives my husband time alone with our daughter before he leaves for work. So there's nothing wrong with my shower practice. It's practical. But Ben's idea is that if we challenge any aspect of our functional fixedness by making a change, we can create a shift in our perceptions, the way a vacation gives us a fresh outlook by taking us away from our normal routine. The change may not be enormous, but it can be potent and useful.

During one of my attempts to get functionally unfixed, I took my shower later in the morning for a week. The first day I got to see the sunrise as I ate my breakfast. It was uplifting. On the second day, when my skin-and-bones toddler wanted cream cheese and jelly on a bagel—which always turns into her licking the jelly off and asking for more—for the first time I realized I could put the cream cheese on top of the jelly instead of the other way around. Sure enough, she ate the high-calorie cream cheese on her way to the jelly. That afternoon I made myself a lunch of sliced egg on toast and I shook the salt and pepper on the bread before I put the egg on top. I liked it much better that way because salt wasn't the first thing I tasted and the pepper didn't burn my lips. These were tiny changes, but they were improvements in my everyday life. The next day I had on my list to print out all the e-mails that were cluttering up my on-line mail folder. I'd been putting off this chore for weeks because it seemed overwhelmingly boring. I looked at the twenty or so files, and suddenly it occurred to me that I could print out three a day over the next week. The shift in the way I saw the work made it manageable.

Our Writing Self gets functionally fixed when it comes to rewriting. We have our attitudes about revision, our ways of doing it, or our reasons not to do it at all. When we challenge just one of these beliefs, we create a shift. By examining your rewriting attitudes you can decide which one you want to change. So, ask yourself these questions: What does revision mean to me? How do I do it? Why do I do it? Your answers will include your functionally fixed concepts. For a fresh perspective on rewriting, challenge one of them your own way, or borrow an outlook about rewriting to try on from my answers to the same three questions.

Question #1: What Is Revision?

I consider revision to be all of what takes place after I set down the first draft of a piece. I also consider revision to be the way to make my thinking and my writing clearer. The most basic definition of revision is to see again. It's a return. When you take the time to return, to experience more than once what you've written, you are looking for something from it—something additional, or a deeper experience of the same thing you saw in the first place. On one level, rewriting is a straightforward practice. You *add* something new to what exists. You *subtract* or remove a section of what you wrote. You *restructure* through reordering lines, paragraphs, plot, ideas. You *shift perspective* by altering a point of view or what you've emphasized. You *replace* one scene or detail with another. These are the basic processes, or tools.

You can't use the tools until your ideas are solidified in the form of tangible words. Then, you can see your draft, like a sculpture, from many angles because your ideas and images are fixed in words; they're embodied. Only then is it possible to move a scene from the beginning of a chapter to the middle, because it now exists in three paragraphs.

You'll best handle your rewriting tools after your ideas are separated from you by your putting them into the form of a draft. Adjusting to this separation is essential to revising with your creative intuition guiding you. We relate to our thoughts differently than we do to written words, just as we use water in a liquid state in a different way from when it's solid ice. When I think about a character, I might have a whole picture in my mind, but once I put her on paper I'm making choices about how I present her: visually first or through dialogue, wide-angled or up-close, gradually or all at once? As Jane Hirshfield points out in *Nine Gates,* historically, it was when humans developed *written* language, instead of relying solely on the spoken word, that we had the ability to fix ideas in time and therefore to examine them in new ways. For instance, when an idea is written down we can reflect on it in relation to the past and the future. Once you understand that in written form your ideas are in a different state and that the new state poses new questions, you come to enjoy your revising tools as much as your computer or your pen.

Revision is also an act of caring for your writing. When you complete a first draft, you've created a base form, the clay. Rewriting is working the clay to make it useful. Revising sculpts the clay into a shape, a vessel that holds and focuses the energy of your ideas and imagery. You want to sculpt the vessel, to make your words powerful enough to thoroughly house what is difficult, painful, or otherwise important to you. But you can only make the vessel strong once you work the stiff clay—that first draft that gives your inspiration solid form. Then revision makes it a home.

The Maggid, or storyteller, Yitzhak Buxbaum uses similar vessel imagery in explaining the point of Jewish spiritual practices. Such observances as regular prayer and adherence to dietary restrictions are meant to prepare you as a vessel, to give your spirit the tools to replicate your individual relationship to God in your relationship to the community. The practices are supposed to influence your spirit so that your dealings with others are holy. In a sense, with writing you revise as a similar practice, to influence and shape the spirit of your words so they speak to others as powerfully as you experienced them when you first related to them in your thoughts.

Like birth, the creation of a first draft is an experience that feels complete in and of itself. But after the birth comes the realization that there is another experience—revision—that is complete in and of itself. After I gave birth to our daughter, my husband and I spent two days in the hospital basking in the glory and miracle of creation. We felt awestruck and exhausted and like we had accomplished a great achievement. Then it was time to go home with our baby. Only at that moment did we fully appreciate that our part in her care had just begun. We have to parent our writing beyond its birth into a first draft as well.

One more way to understand the value of revision is as a form of civilizing our writing. To some people, civilization is as questionable as rewriting. Many of us tend to mistrust the element of taming that they share. But it's only in relation to civilization that we are able to appreciate certain aspects of the wild. I'm thinking about an essay by Sy Safransky, activist and editor of the literary journal *The Sun,* about going camping with his wife. Safransky writes that he knows he's supposed to be able to experience the sacredness of the wilderness. He recognizes the aspects of the landscape that should feed his soul. But he is miserable despite his understanding because he's uncomfortable and afraid without a soft bed, protection from the elements of danger, running water. He comes to realize that he can't really do without civilization. It isn't, after all, someone else's mistake that he's forced to live with. He gladly relies on civilization. With writing, as well, we may be able to recognize the wild and sacred elements of our words, but we may not be able to fully benefit from them until we civilize them by refining or revising them.

Finally, I often think of revision as translation. The translator's job is to change a communication from its original language into another. She makes a series of choices in order to convey the meaning, tone, flow, and essence of the words in their new language. It is a process of exchanges and negotiation. For instance, if the original words include a concept for which there is no word in the new language, the translator must decide on an approximation even if the substitute changes the rhythm of the passage. In rewriting, the language of the first draft is like the translator's original text. It's the language that you used to solidify your thoughts in writing. So in a first draft, you might say, "The night was beautiful," and leave it at that because you have a vivid picture in your mind of the night and you were struck by its allure. In revising, however, you would translate the word "beautiful" so that someone who didn't have an image of that night already in his mind could, from your description, picture it and be affected by its beauty. The first language is what you used to turn your thoughts into words, and the new language is what you use to express them beyond yourself.

However you approach revision, without its structure, the energy of our writing can dissipate, leaving us wanting more from our words than they provide. Our written words crave the kind of form that rewriting provides as deeply as we are driven to create structure for the rest of our lives through our work, hobbies, and the rituals we participate in. Even if there are aspects of the revision process you find troubling, revising is as much a part of respecting your Writing Self as are the parts of the creative process you already love. With this understanding of rewriting, it's time to consider the best way for you to approach it.

Question #2: How Do You Revise?

First and foremost, you revise by being open to the process and by believing in its import. Then you discover the ways to do it that pique your interest, that sound like fun, and that inspire you. A sense of obligation toward revising probably won't nourish you. It'll tax your Writing Self rather than energize it. What follows are several suggestions for approaching revision. Maybe one will work for you or perhaps suggest another way for you to enter the rewriting process. If not, at least you will know that there are many options and that somewhere out there is the one for you.

APPROACHING REVISION AS LOVER

Writer Hal Zina Bennet describes the importance of a writer's relationship to both real and imagined readers. The distinction between the two kinds of readers is the difference between the audience you write for: athletes, social activists, or carpenters; and the person or people who inspired you to write your piece in the first place: your mother before she was a married woman with children, the driver who cut you off last week, a younger you, or yourself right now. My imaginary reader for this book is someone I met at a writing conference.

When you consider your reader, one way to return to a piece of writing in order to revise it is by casting yourself in the role of your reader's lover. Your see your reader, whether real or imaginary, as the Dear One whom you want to touch and excite. How you excite your reader will vary. You may need to be a gentle lover in the way in which you approach your subject and in your tone. You may want to be a fierce lover, laying your message on the line in raw and immediate language. Either way, when you go back to your first draft, call your reader to mind. See him or her fully; spend a few moments together in thought or in writing in your journal and then reread your draft with this lover at your side, gauging your words by his response, her arousal. As Bennet says, as a lover you must love your reader as much as you love your writing.

STRUCTURE: APPROACHING REVISION AS THE EXPLORER

Structure is at the heart of a great deal of revision work. Structure is often more apparent to writers who have been steeped in a landscape, a tradition, a lifestyle, or a culture from a young age because the rhythms and cycles of these elements are part of their sensibility that extends into how they order and present their writing. If you, like me, have lived several lifestyles or in many places, structure may not be as obvious or ingrained in your sensibility. It will require effort to decide on a structure. Effort can mean actively seeking out structures for your writings or being still and paying attention to your surroundings.

Think about revision as a quest for the best structure for the piece you're writing. Your role is that of the explorer, the seeker, the investigator. You begin revision as a treasure hunter, poised to recognize what makes your piece whole. Your mission is to discover the proverbial missing half of the golden amulet or a route to a new world. Your path is full of clues, such as conversations you overhear, the evening news, advice from writing books. Some of them are dead ends, while others bring you closer to a firm shape for your piece. Your job is to take note of all the clues and learn which are the true ones.

As an explorer, you might first look for a new way to structure your piece in likely places, such as in the writing of those you admire. You might, for example, experiment with the diary form you love so much in a novel you've recently read. Then you might search out the unlikely places to discover structures for your work by considering such patterns as those you find in landscaped gardens, in the best days of your life, in the way you observe that a bee travels. As an investigator, all your revising options are clues for you to piece together in order to solve the mystery of structure and discover the treasure that is your finished piece.

APPROACHING REVISION WITH SMALL ADJUSTMENTS

When revising feels overwhelming, keep in mind that great changes are often born from small adjustments. Rewriting is more than copy-editing, i.e., correcting spelling and grammar, checking references, and making sure sentences make sense, but still, for some of us it's best to start with the smallest, most rudimentary changes.

As a student of yoga, I often find myself straining in a pose until the class instructor says something like, "In a side bend, try to stretch the side you're bending as much as the side you're stretching," or "When you stand, share the weight of your body with your little toes." When I make these small adjustments, the strain disappears, the pose opens up, and my breath flows freely through my body.

Bring this practice of making small adjustments into revision. Your Writing Self is a subtle being and therefore may sometimes first need a subtle change in order to shift into the rewriting process. As you make one small adjustment at a time, you set in motion a domino effect that leads to the larger steps of revising. Small starts include changing the perspective of the piece from first to third person, for example, or altering the weather, making the last line the first line or vice versa, giving one of your central characters a favorite song. Or try reading your piece aloud and noting where you hesitate or feel tight in your voice as you read. Mark those spots and then go back to make one small adjustment to each of them.

APPROACHING REVISION AS PLAY

Another rewriting lesson I learned from yoga was not to force changes. My teacher would constantly remind us not to strain ourselves when attempting a pose because the stress and strain we put on ourselves undermines the pose's benefits. Rather than pushing us to go beyond our limits, yoga encourages us to play with using our breath to relax into the poses, to soften. Applying this idea to rewriting, when I feel stuck or unmotivated, I use the opposite of force in order to revise. I become playful and experimental as I approach a section that baffles me. I might open up the dictionary and randomly choose a word and see if I can relate it to, or use it in, the section I'm working on. Or I'll purposely write in very lofty language or slang or clichés for a while, deliberately making the passage worse! Often these little detours make me laugh and relax, which in turn allows me to enjoy revising again.

APPROACHING REVISION AS CHOREOGRAPHER AND CONSTRUCTIVIST

The period of my life that I spent studying and practicing choreography taught me another way to approach revision. In fact, it is through my work as a choreographer that the rewriting aspect of my Writing Self was rejuvenated. A choreographer has, as a medium, powerful dancers in the way that a writer has access to powerful words. A choreographer develops a group of movement phrases for her dancers to perform in the way that a writer has in mind a set of ideas for her words to embody. The work of the choreographer is to combine dancers and movements into a series of patterns in a performance space. The work of a writer is to combine words and ideas in a series of patterns on the page. When I choreograph a dance, I experiment with movement phrases on my dancers the way I try out my ideas in words. I group both dancers and words in various combinations. Seeing my movements performed by dancers suggests more patterns and other movements and combinations for them to try. Reading my ideas in a draft suggests other words and combinations of words to incorporate into the piece. This is how my dances and my writings evolve; I revise my movements and my ideas as I see them embodied in the dancers and the words, each one shaping and reshaping the dance or the draft.

My visual art develops in the same way. I'm categorized as a Constructivist in the realm of art, which means that I co-create my pieces by using objects that already exist. My work brings familiar elements into new relationships with one another. For example, one sculpture, *License to Choose*, takes the name of a controversial birth control pill, RU486, and presents it on the kind of license plate we have on our cars. At the time I created it, there was a question as to whether this pill would be licensed for legal distribution in America. Through listening to the essence of the word "license," I discovered how I would convey my feelings about the controversy visually. Mine is revisionist art. The rewriting process is similar in that we use familiar words in refreshing relationships in order to express our ideas. The co-creative approach in writing or in making art requires the ability to pay attention to the essence of words or objects.

In a draft of an essay, I might find an awkwardly written paragraph and focus in on a few central words or phrases. Then I pay close attention to them, opening myself up to the images and associations they bring to mind. Often a stronger, clearer way to get my idea across comes from this process. As an artist, I shape my ideas and images using objects the way I revise the original language of a first draft in writing. You may find parallel forms for revising your writing in other activities from your life as well.

There is such a wide range of rewriting techniques available to you; at one end of the spectrum, author Jack Hodgins believes that referring to your current draft at all prevents your imagination from being free enough to resee your piece. Hodgins suggests that you are being an editor instead of a writer if you revise with a copy of the first draft in front of you. He considers a previous draft to be more like a guide to consult and put away before you start another draft from a position of "relaxed confidence." On the other end of the revision spectrum, some people revise methodically in two phases. The first time, they rewrite the content of their piece, the ideas. The second time, they revise, they let the content stand and pay attention to the form: the order of sentences, paragraphs, ideas, events, scenes, and chapters.

Question #3: Why Revise?

Whether or not you've found a stimulating, intriguing revising perspective, a motivating reason to do it will help you stay enthused, focused, and purposeful. And in asking yourself the question Why revise at all? you're sure to ferret out and then be able to challenge your functionally fixed ideas about revision.

So why do *you* do it? With what attitude do you do it? How do you know when to stop? Earlier I said that revision is a return. The written world allows us to capture our ideas and revisit them exactly as we initially recorded them. Even beyond the world of writing, return is an essential component of experiencing completeness. Think of all the rituals of return we practice and hold dear: our annual faith ceremonies and rituals, the telling and passing on of stories, going back to visit one's hometown.

When you return to a piece of writing, you invest more time and energy in it. In the process of making it better, you enrich yourself. You gain greater understanding of what your piece is about because the writing has a longer time to act on you, to reach you more deeply. Perhaps you feel the same would be true if you simply reread the piece without changing it. But then your enrichment would be passive, similar to rereading a favorite book, instead of including the active, participatory richness of rewriting. After all, the way to keep knowledge you receive is to act on it.

Another reason to revise is to honor the relationship between the writer and the reader, even if you are one and the same. You're affirming that what you wrote is worthy of return, has something deep to offer, is a gift you're honored to give. It's arrogant to ask your reader to give full attention to something that you yourself aren't willing to take time to fully absorb. It's like inviting someone for dinner, opening a can of chili, and serving it cold in a chipped bowl when there's a baked salmon and new potatoes in your oven and china in the cabinets. You revise with the intention of being a fitting partner to your reader.

As a practice, rewriting uses parts of the Writing Self that aren't fully engaged through percolation, first drafts, or going public; one of them is a keener aspect of your intellect that allows you to rework your ideas or deepen them. Revising exercises writing and thinking muscles that don't get used otherwise. Working one set of muscles strengthens related muscle groups, too.

Another benefit of revision is that it tends to tone you down. Paying such close attention to individual words and phrases or to the flow of a passage helps you to stay focused at a subtler level that sophisticates your capacity for reflection and for noticing the extraordinary in the commonplace. It becomes natural for you to think at a deeper level. As Thomas Moore points out, bringing precision to your written words carries over into making you less complacent in your thinking in general as well. As a result, you are empowered to act on what you think and believe. Your words become more dimensional. You and your characters start to resist getting mired in generalizations such as feeling "sad"; instead you feel melancholy, devalued, or disappointed. Such clarity and exactness animates life. This aspect of revision is one reason why writing can be a path to emotional healing.

There are even three good metaphysical reasons to revise. The first arises from cutting out sections of your piece. For some of us, it's a painful process to remove passages or even whole chapters that we're attached to. It feels like a kind of sacrifice, which it is. But to gain something larger, like a piece of writing that resonates beyond ourselves, we must often let go of something smaller, like our feelings about a particular section.

The second visionary reason to revise is as a practice that opens us to what mystic David Spangler calls the Mystery. Spangler says that reasoned thinking and critical discernment, which are faculties we use when rewriting, are necessary aspects of our ability to be receptive to invisible domains such as inspiration and imagination. You may have an illuminating idea buried in a bunch of tangled-up sentences, an idea you might only be dimly aware of. If you haven't developed the skills to extract it or clarify it, it can't enlighten anyone—including you. So if we continually ignore revision, we may deprive ourselves of access to a level of our own wisdom and creativity.

Finally, rewriting helps us to do with our writing what spiritual tradition asks us to do in prayer: to ask for blessings for the whole world, not just for our particular community. Revising is one way we prepare our writing to go beyond ourselves, whether by sharing it publicly or by revising to extend our own understanding of what we write.

To revise with enthusiasm and passion, forget what a demanding inner critic may hiss; rewriting isn't the impossible task of perfecting something. It's a practice, and in this case practice isn't supposed to make perfect; practice makes completion.

Practice

∼ NUTS AND BOLTS: PRACTICAL REVISING TECHNIQUES

There is both a very practical aspect to developing revising skills and an aspect that has more to do with shifting your perspective about doing it. First you need a collection of effective day-to-day rewriting tools and techniques to get you started when you're ready to revise. I suggest using the first two practices every time you revise and the others on an as-needed basis.

1. Voice Activated

This first practice will help you to determine what sections of your piece need to be revised. Your own voice will be your guide. Through using this exercise as an initial revising process for all your pieces, you'll also develop an ever-deepening trust in your voice as a writer and a speaker.

Read your piece aloud with pen in hand and, if possible, a tape recorder on. Mark places as you go that are difficult to read because you lose your train of thought or you stumble over words or phrases or you have to stop mid-sentence in order to take a breath. As much as you can, don't interrupt the flow of reading. Just flag the awkward spots with an X. Next, put your draft aside and listen to your recording with a blank piece of paper and a pen at your side. On the paper, using key words or reminder phrases, note where your voice falters or your own attention to the piece drifts away as you're listening. Each of the spots you've marked is a place in your draft to revise. When you are ready to actually revise the sections you've noted, go back to each awkward passage and read it aloud again at least twice to help you hear and remember what caused you to consider rewriting it.

2. Pick a Card, Any Card

Once you've decided what sections to revise, the next step is to choose what to do to improve them. Sometimes the answer is obvious, such as when a sentence goes on for so long that you can't say it in a single breath or you read a passage that doesn't even make sense to you, the author of the words. But often we have more of a feeling that something is out of kilter in a section without knowing what it is, or we see what the problem is but we don't know how to fix it. When you feel stumped is the time to try serendipity as a revising method.

To start the revision process from an open and effortless position,

on separate small cards write each of the following words: add, subtract, restructure, shift perspective, replace. Put these in a bowl, close
your eyes, pick one, and do whatever the card says to do to the sections
of your draft that need work. Alternatively, for each problematic section in your first draft, pick a different card and see how you can help
the section using the card's method. It may appear that these techniques aren't deliberate or thoughtful enough because they rely on
chance as opposed to critical evaluation. Yet because the most satisfying experience of revision comes from allowing your intuition and
inspiration to guide you rather than your critical abilities, these
approaches support a similar type of spontaneity that helps you recognize aspects of your writing that you might not otherwise notice. If
you want more control of the process, a third plan is to post the card
phrases and their definitions (see pp. 81–82) above your writing space.
As you reread each problematic section of your draft, refer to your list
and pick the rewriting action to take that makes the most sense to you.

3. New Eyes

Sometimes the issue with a piece isn't so much particular sections
of the writing as that, as a whole, the piece feels off, lacking in energy
or momentum. When you're sure your idea is sound and the plot or
progression makes sense yet your draft has little power, there are several possibilities. You might need to give yourself more time and distance from the piece before you're able to see what's missing. It might
be that the piece isn't one that you're meant to go much further with.
Or you need a new perspective on it in order to move forward.
Whichever of the above turns out to be the case, try this technique
before you decide whether to file the draft away for later, chuck it, or
keep revising it.

Rewrite your piece in the present, the future, or the past tense.
Or change the point of view into first person ("I"), second person
("you"), or third person ("she"). This exercise gives you a fresh angle

on the draft that can energize you to revise even if you don't stick with the new tense or point of view. You may also discover what's missing from the original version because it is more obvious in the new one. But if the new version feels as flat as the first, save both to reread in a month's time and decide then whether or not to keep revising.

4. Scissors

I practice and preach this next technique because creativity isn't linear. This practice uses your intuitive abilities in a playful way. It helps with both revising the structure of your draft and generating more material. Time and again I've written drafts of poems, essays, and longer works that are almost entirely complete, except that the sentences that contain the ideas are out of order. By "order" I mean a progression that makes sense to a reader, or makes it possible for the reader to follow my thoughts. For instance, a sentence that clarifies a thought in my first paragraph might appear in the midst of my third paragraph. When I put my writing in a more orderly progression I see aspects of my ideas that I don't notice in initial drafts.

Using your latest draft, with a scissors, cut up your piece into separate paragraphs, sentences, stanzas, or lines. On the back of each, number the sections in their original order. Place all the sections in a pile on the floor or put them in their original sequence and play with rearranging the order. What if the opening paragraph was the last, or vice versa? If the results give you more ideas about the piece, write your new ideas on loose paper that you can add and integrate into your cut-up draft. If turning the opening paragraph into the final one made the draft stronger, put a number marking the paragraph's new position on its face. Keep working this way until you have either a new order that you like or enough new material for you to write a whole new draft that includes it.

It's very important that you do this exercise with hard copy. It doesn't work on the computer. It's the kinesthetic experience of actually moving your ideas around with your hands that engages your intuitive abilities.

5. Start Over

At some point, everyone gets involved with a writing project in which they become mired in rewriting. Use this technique if you've been working on the same piece of writing for too long, meaning you've written an inordinate number of drafts of it or you've been tinkering with the same draft forever. Since the number of drafts that is standard differs from writer to writer, you'll have to judge for yourself if you are at the point of needing help to move on. You can also use this technique with a draft for which you've gotten a lot of feedback from a writing teacher, class, or writing group.

Reread the drafts and all the comments, then put them away and start your piece anew, trusting that your psyche will synthesize the drafts and commentaries into the new piece. But no looking back! The idea is to trust your soupy psyche. If you want to try this with a book-length work, read one entire draft of the manuscript first and then, as you are rewriting, reread each chapter once again before you put it away and start fresh.

6. Less Is More

When revising just seems too overwhelming, start by making only one small adjustment to your piece that isn't under the copyediting category (spelling, grammar, punctuation). Instead change something that will affect the content: Change the weather against which the piece or scene is set, give the main character a pet. Once you've made the change, go back and read your draft again and notice the effect of the change, not just on the draft but on your ability to keep revising.

One small rewriting action often propels you past resistances and obstacles to revising. As you read over the draft, mark any places that you now feel ready to rewrite. If you notice sections that seem to need work but you feel something akin to exhaustion at the prospect of doing it, skip that section for now. Don't even put a mark beside it. Instead work only on what you feel up to. Continue to revise by chunking down the process into small, manageable parcels, putting off the most inscrutable sections. As a result of all the rest of the rewriting you do on the draft, those difficult sections may no longer need much revising, or having accomplished the rest of the revising, you will have developed more confidence and stamina to tackle the tough parts. If the one small adjustment you made initially didn't provide you with the momentum to keep on rewriting, then try the technique again by making another small adjustment.

➷ REVISE YOUR PERSPECTIVE ON REVISING

The five practices that follow reexamine revising. The techniques will help you to clarify your revising attitudes so you can shift the ones that don't serve you and supplement the perspectives that work for you.

1. Inventory

To take the pulse of your current relationship to revising, answer the following questions in writing. Feel free to write in list, phrase, or full-sentence form, whichever works best for you.

What does revision mean to you?
How do you do it?
Why do you do it?

Consider your responses carefully. Is there something you've written that keeps you from fully embracing revision? If so, use any combination of the exercises below to help you change your outlook.

2. Hidden Gains

Once you know what your resistances to rewriting are, make a list of what you have to gain by avoiding revising. To make such a list is tricky. You're essentially asking yourself the question, What else in my writing life don't I have to confront by avoiding revision? Your answers might include not having to try publishing or not having to commit too deeply to your subject or ideas. Once you've nailed down these insights into why you avoid revision, you can begin to challenge them. If, for instance, your fear of publishing comes up in this exercise, you could give yourself a year from completing your first revised piece to even have to address your fears, much less actually making your writing public. The point of finding the hidden gains of not revising is to stop you from postponing rewriting, not to give you a new reason to put it off, such as, I can't revise until I resolve my publishing fears.

3. Unfix Yourself

Challenging your functional fixedness will support any change you want to make in your relationship to revising by shifting your overall outlook on your routines. For five days do something different or out of order in your writing routine or your regular life. For example, journal for ten minutes after you write; write only humor; write in a different location or with a pencil instead of a pen or your computer; switch fonts; eat only vegetarian food; choose a different route to work. Make note of any changes in your view of your writing or your life over the five days and for the week that follows. Look them over for one you can incorporate into your perspective on revision. When I realized that I could spread jelly on a bagel under the cream cheese to get my daughter to eat it, I carried the insight into a manuscript I was writing at the time. I stopped trying to fix a troublesome chapter to make it fit where I'd placed it, and instead I moved it deeper into the middle of the manuscript. Until the bagel, reordering the chapter hadn't occurred to me as a revising solution.

4. Take the Lead

As I've mentioned, a person's distaste for revision is often caused by the inner critical voice leading the rewriting process rather than the intuitive voice being leader and the critic following as servant. This exercise, which is especially good for visual learners, helps put the twins Critic and Creator in a proper relationship to each other as you revise.

Find or make your own evocative images of the god and goddess Critic and Intuition, using pictures from magazines, old photos, your own drawings, found objects. If you close your eyes, how would these beings look? Malevolent? Benign? Curious? Serene? Paste your images on a piece of paper above your writing space or prop them up as part of your writing altar. Be sure to place them in relation to one another as they're meant to be—Critic in service to Creator/Intuition. Look at them as you revise and see how having physical images of them affects your attitude and approach to revision.

5. Don't Try

Unconsciously accepting the conventional wisdom that it's hard to revise can cause your negativity about doing it. Use this practice to counter the prevailing message as well as anytime you struggle with rewriting.

Rewrite a section of a piece without trying, whatever "trying" means to you. (It may mean scrutinizing every sentence, or graphing the plot, or adding lively verbs, or attempting to make the piece "better.") In other words, give up whatever you feel you're supposed to do when you rewrite or whatever seems hard to do and approach the draft with no other intention than to see what else happens when you return to it with pen in hand. You won't be able to rely on this practice to completely revise a section. But if you use it as a warm-up, a way to begin each revising session, you will revise without hunched-up shoulders or a furrowed brow and without all the stressful attitudes about revising that accompany them.

∾ TRY ON SOMETHING NEW

The next five practices are techniques for cultivating replacement or additional perspectives on revising. The exercises are experiments with a variety of outlooks on revision. Pick one that appeals to you, or try all of them. Each one will give you practice with a revising perspective I offer people who are looking for a new approach to rewriting.

1. Lover

Revise with your reader in mind as a lover. Pick one piece you're working on and reread it. Take a few moments to close your eyes and call up the image of your reader—either the person who prompted you to write the piece in the first place or the person you imagine reading it when it's done (they might be the same person). When you have a firm picture of the person in your mind, including the expression on his face and the position of his body (standing, sitting, slouching, etc.), open your eyes and read the piece again, aloud, to this reader. Next, journal in the form of a dialogue with your imaginary reader about either the piece itself or whatever else you each wish to discuss before your next rewriting session.

As a way to get started on a dialogue with your reader in your journal, ask him questions such as, What else do you want to know? What do you think? You can comment to your reader about your impressions of how he responded to the draft, you can talk a bit about your own impressions and feelings. Keep your side of the dialogue brief because your goal is to hear the most you can from your reader. Pay attention to the tone your reader speaks in. Is it demanding? Calm? Tentative? When you revise, be sure to gauge the tone of your words so that they bring out the emotional response you want from your reader, based on your experience in the journal dialogue with him. If he sounded agitated, make your words soothing. If she was bullying, don't give in.

2. *Structure and Exploration*

To rewrite as an explorer, experiment with two different ways to structure a section of your draft or an entry from your journal. Choose patterns or structures you notice in nature or in machinery. The > formation of flying birds, for example, might suggest starting from a very general description and going on to be more specifically detailed. Or the rotation of two connecting gears might suggest a way of narrating two events in the same chapter, scene, or poem so that the actions line up in relation to one another. Not every pattern you try will improve your piece. But just by exercising your writing in this way you will widen the frontier of your choices, which in turn will broaden your capacity to notice what your draft needs.

3. *Translation*

Whenever I can, I invite people to experiment with revision as an act of translation. It's an especially good practice for those of us who get strongly attached to our words as we first write them down. Translators often have the job of selecting the words in their own language that best represent the meaning and nuances of the word in its original language. When the purpose of the original language is to turn pure thought into words, as the translator, our job is to find alternative words and phrases that make our meaning more accessible to others. To warm up to the process of revising your own writing as a translator, first try translating others. Read the following two translations of "Les Chats" by Baudelaire. Then create a third version of your own by taking what you like from the first two and combining them. As you do this, notice your preferences.

CATS (translated by Michael Becker)

Ardent lovers and austere scholars
Love to an equal degree in their later years,
Powerful and gentle cats, pride of the house,
Who, like them, are shivery and sedentary.

Friends of knowledge and of sensuousness
They seek silence and the terror of darkness;
Erèbe might have used them as its funeral messengers
If their pride would suffer such bondage.

They assume dreamily the noble bearing
Of the great sphinxes stretched out in the depths of solitude
Which seem to sleep in an endless dream.

Their fertile loins burst with magic sparks,
And flecks of gold, like fine sand,
Hazily stud their eyes.

THE CATS *(translated by Julie Convisser)*

Fervent lovers or ascetics,
whether powerful, gentle, oblivious, or cold,
all fever like cats
in the mating season.

Scientists and hedonists alike
seek silence and annihilation,
the proud death
that follows the love cry.

They may appear as the noble sphinx,
thoughtful, langorous in his solitude,
in a dream without end.

But their loins spark and burn
inside their sleek fur—
see the fire in their eyes.

Did you choose lines in which the meanings were clearer or in which they were more open-ended? Did the rhythm and tone of a line affect your decision more than or as much as the meaning? Did you find yourself supplying your own version of a line by combining aspects of the two you could choose from? Both English versions are translations of the very same poem. In the first translation, "loins burst with magic sparks." In the second, they "spark and burn." Each version conveys the power of the loins, but the first relates the power to an explosion of a mystical nature and the second to an igniting and consumption. Perhaps the French encompasses both ideas, and the translators chose according to what was closer to each one's own experience. The next time you rewrite a piece of your own, remember this exercise and think of your draft as something someone else has written and that you now must translate into a language that new people will understand and appreciate.

4. Sound and Light

One of the final steps in the revision process, a step that often makes the difference between a strong piece of writing and an exceptional one, is attending to the music and texture of your words, their sound and rhythm. It's at this fundamental and subliminal level that language, and the ideas that it carries, can penetrate us most deeply. When words sing they captivate us.

You don't have to go over every word you've written with a thesaurus in hand to create music in your writing. However, by reading a draft aloud, paragraph by paragraph, you can, for instance, find synonyms for words you repeat often, and those synonyms can be ones that support the tone of the paragraph by their sound or by the associations they inspire. For example, if you have used the phrase "stems from" several times to explain that one idea comes from another, you might find an especially suitable substitute such as the word "arises," which supports the image of one idea growing out of another. At the same time, musically, "arises" is a word in which the second syllable springs out of the first the way the ideas you're writing about come from one another. Even if you change only a handful of words in this way, you will be infusing your draft with music and texture. The more you tune in to this level of words, the more natural it becomes to revise this way.

To focus on revising at the subtle level of the sound and rhythm of words, pick out poetry in a language you are unfamiliar with and translate it into English. Try this exercise at least once. The more often you do it, the better you'll get at integrating music and texture into your writing. The point here is not to get your translation right in the sense of guessing correctly what the foreign words actually mean. The point is to use the unknown to temporarily get away from the definition of words so that you can focus on their sound first. With this in mind, base your translation on what the words sound like they might mean, on your associations to them. For this exercise, don't get caught up in such fine points as whether your translated version makes sense! But do choose a poem in a language that already has at least some overlap in English, such as German or a Romance language. Before you begin writing down translated words, read the whole poem aloud to the best of your ability, so you can hear the words you'll be translating. It will help you make your associations in English. For a taste of this exercise, translate the following section of Dadaist poet Hugo Ball's poem *Karawane,* which is in an entirely made-up, nonsense language. For instance, I've seen the title *Karawane* translated into English as caravan, carafe of wine, and Kara's whining.

KARAWANE

Yolifanto bamble
o fali bambla
grossinga heje

Some people become enchanted by this exercise. For others it is nearly impossible to switch over into approaching words this way, without their denotative meanings. Either way, it's a worthwhile exercise to translate poems in a language you don't know, based on the sounds and associations you make with the words. The effect will be that when you revise your writing you will start to include the process of refining the sounds, textures, and rhythms of your word choices.

5. Your Own Backyard

Your own fresh perspective on revision may lie in a hobby or a passion in your life unrelated to writing that suggests ways to reframe your outlook on revision. For instance, if you garden, try gardening with revising in mind. Relate the way in which you pinch back new growth so the plant will use its energy for fuller blossoms or a fuller shape to the process of cutting back sections of your piece to make it stronger. If you swim, you might relate the way you adjust the timing of your stroke so that it's in sync with your breathing to adjusting the length of a scene you've written so that it better supports the story's progression to its climax.

Start this process by choosing a hobby or passion to examine. Write a list of all the discrete actions or aspects of the activity. A gardening list would include tilling, planting, weeding, pruning, and so on. Look over your list for any obvious correlations between one of the actions and an aspect of rewriting and write down the connection beside the action: pruning—cutting back sections of a passage to make it shapely. The next three times you are engaged in your hobby or passion, think about revision as you do it and see if any other connections occur to you. If so, add them to your list. You don't have to come up with a one-to-one correspondence between all the actions of your hobby and all the aspects of revision for the connection to be valid or helpful to your rewriting process. Post the list in your writing area, and while you revise, refer to it occasionally by simply reading over the list and waiting a few moments to see if something from it resonates with you as a method of rewriting the draft you're working on.

Body-Mind Exercise

∾ *SONG AND DANCE*

This exercise will reignite your revision process when you're feeling contracted and stagnant and you need an inspiring jolt. You set your revision process in motion physically. The concept behind this approach is that whatever you experience with your body will translate to your mind. When you're bodily awake to revising, it infiltrates your psyche. This exercise is based on Joscelyn Godwin's book *The Mystery of the Seven Vowels,* in which he suggests that vowel sounds penetrate our bodies and compel emotionally expressive movement in us.

Choose one of the following vowels: a, e, o, u. Close your eyes and repeat the vowel as one continuous sound (ahahahahahahahahaha-hah), stopping only to get your breath and begin again. As you make the vowel sound, start to move your arms and/or your body in whatever way the sound suggests to you, such as lifting your arms to the sky, embracing yourself, shaking your head. Don't stop until you've done your movement many times over as you chant the vowel. Repeat this exercise once with each vowel. Be sure to rest for a while and to breathe normally for at least five minutes before beginning to work with a new vowel.

List the emotion and the expressive movement you experienced for each vowel. When you lifted your arms to the sky, did you feel vulnerable? Or expansive? Post your list in your writing area. Now, with your body memory of how even a vowel can inspire emotion and gestures, reread a sentence, passage, or paragraph you're trying to revise and make up a physical movement to express it. If the passage is about driving, is your movement relaxed? Or intent? Or nervous? Repeat the movement a few times and sit down again to rewrite.

The list you made from the vowel-chant exercise will come in handy while you're revising an especially emotional passage. Scan the passage for how often you use words with the vowel sound that corresponds to the primary emotion of the section. Get up and make the vowel sound and the accompanying physical movements before continuing to revise the passage.

∽ LET THE CHILD BALANCE YOU

If you tend to be critical or contemptuous toward your draft or your Writing Self as you revise, restore balance between the Critic and the Creator by spending time in Child's Pose, a hatha yoga posture. On a comfortable surface, preferably a carpeted floor, get on your hands and knees, then guide your rear end toward the floor between your legs. Now rest your forehead on the floor and, keeping your palms in touch with the floor, stretch your arms beyond your head until they're as straight as possible without being rigid. Start taking deep breaths. On the inhale, feel your shoulder blades separate like two sides of a book when it's opened. On the exhale, feel those same muscles relax. Do this a few times.

Now, inhale breath into your lower back, and on the exhale feel those lower back muscles release on either side of your spine. Do this a few times. Keep breathing deeply. During the inhale, imagine your intuition is housed on one side of your spine and your intellect on the other. During the exhale, feel them both relaxing and releasing beside each other.

Now, keeping your palms in contact with the floor, bring your arms to your sides and turn your palms faceup, resting the backs of your hands and wrists against the floor beside your thighs. Inhale and exhale deeply, filling your intuition and intellect with breath and releasing tension, feeling both aspects of yourself in service to your words, your writing, your spine. When you're ready, come out of the pose slowly. Now, when your Critic overtakes the rewriting process, take a deep breath, pulling air into your whole back area while imagining the Creator and the Critic being balanced, calibrated, on either side of your spine by the breath you're inhaling and exhaling.

WHEN ALL ELSE FAILS

If you just can't bring yourself to feel remotely enthusiastic about revising or even open to it, back up and try to create mental space in your psyche for the possibility of revising. Approaching revision from a physical angle could be your last best chance.

Sit on the floor in any position that you find comfortable. Gently rock side to side in order to feel your sitz bones. You might even pull the flesh of your buttocks behind you to help you really feel the bones. Now, breathe into the trunk of your body. As you breathe, let your belly be loose. Breathe with the intention of making space, making room for all your organs to be comfortable: liver, kidneys, intestines, stomach, gallbladder, reproductive organs.

Now, take several inhalations and exhalations to guide your breath up your spine, and a few more up the back of your neck and into your head. Feel a space for revising opening up in that 90 percent of your brain that we don't yet understand. Continue to guide your breath to the crown of your head, to where your soft spot was when you were a baby. Don't worry if you don't know exactly where it is, just pick the point that feels right to you. Imagine that soft spot gently reopening. Once it's open, spend a couple of minutes aware of yourself in this state of receptivity. Your body is full of space for your organs. Your sitz bones are separated and open.

Breathe deeply and feel your whole body as a vessel with room, with space. Without having to know exactly what it is, invite the essence of what will nourish revising to enter you by reaching up to you from the earth or by pouring down to you from the atmosphere. Let any negative thoughts and unseen problematic aspects of your writing drain away. Breathe this way several times until you're ready to become aware of the room again and to open your eyes.

Do the same visualization with a draft you want to revise as you've just done with your body. Start rewriting with the intention of creating a vessel with plenty of space for all the sections to work together. As you sit at your desk, sensate ideas entering through your soft spot and sitz bones, and imagine what needs to be drained from the draft funneling out from the same places. If you feel stuck or frustrated as you rewrite, close your eyes for a few moments and return to this visualization and the sensations that accompany it before you start revising again.

Ten

DON'T REVISE

Now that you know all the excellent reasons to revise, you should also know the excellent reasons not to revise. Most writers don't rewrite every first draft. Sometimes we lose interest in a particular piece. Another inspiration may press harder and take precedence. Or through completing the first draft, we may feel finished with a subject.

There are also rare, spectacular instances when something we write comes out whole the very first time. In more than twenty-five years of writing, I've had a total of maybe a dozen poems and essays come through me this way. It's thrilling, almost miraculous. Often you just know it when a piece is born complete. Otherwise, over time or by sharing it, you discover that the writing is fully realized. If you sit back and wait for these inspired pieces to be channeled through you, you probably don't need to revise your work. But most of us do the majority of our writing between these gifts.

One reason to decide not to revise is that your piece has the single purpose to either record, release, or clarify an emotion or an experience for yourself. If you're writing in order to record a trip you once took or a traumatic experience, what's important is who you were then and what was happening to that you. Revising that piece would defeat the purpose of recording it to begin with. When you write for the sake of emotional release, it's like a wail of joy or grief. It's the momentary catharsis or celebration that matters, and changing your words dilutes their significance and power. If you're writing to clarify something for yourself, for example, journaling for self-awareness, then what's essential is the way the writing slows down and captures your thoughts so that you can focus on and examine them. Revising would compromise the very reason you're writing.

I wrote a piece about eighteen years ago that I call my Cain poem. It came out in one fell swoop. It's powerful to me because it articulates a certain dynamic in my life. It's a personal poem. I have no desire to share it with others or to clarify its rough, shadowy phrases. But I know it by heart, and it helps to remind me to take care of myself without my ever having revised it.

There are reasons to postpone revising as well. One reason is if you finish a first draft but the draft isn't finished with you. There are pieces we write that need to resonate exclusively with us for a while before we can get enough distance from them to rewrite. With poems I write, I often need a long time to absorb the impact of my own words on myself before I can do the work of revising them so that they speak to others. I've written poems about the end of a relationship months ahead of the breakup, but I could revise them only months after the parting of ways. When one of my students has trouble rewriting, the first thing we explore is whether there are aspects to his piece that hold a message he still needs to accept. An example is one student who wrote a short story about being molested. After her attack, the main character immediately encounters a counselor who helps her. This seemed too coincidental in the story, even though in reality it was exactly what had happened to my student. But she couldn't figure out how to change the events to read more plausibly until she had reflected further on what it meant to her that such a fortuitous meeting took place in the wake of such terror.

It's a good idea not to start rewriting the day after you receive feedback on a piece. It takes time for the comments others make to mellow until they don't feel like either an attack or proof that you can't write well. Without a few days or weeks away from the feedback, you might become overwhelmed or frustrated by the sheer number of suggestions and give up on the draft entirely or hack it to bits.

You don't want to overwork your material through revising, either. Poet Eavan Boland is adamant about the danger of losing the integrity and energy of your original idea in revision. She believes that your first words contain the passion of a poem, and she counsels her students to be loyal to them and not to radically alter them. It is possible to rewrite a piece to death. This is a good reason to treat rewriting with restraint.

The best reason to stop revising is your state of mind as you approach your draft. Just as vigorous exercise is good for your physical body but can overtax you when you're feeling ill, stressed, or too tired, in the written world, the exercise of rewriting can adversely affect your Writing Self when you're in the throes of a mind-set I refer to as the Fevers. The Fevers manifest on their own when you're in an especially vulnerable state, or they can be caused by other people, such as an editor who gives you too much feedback or gives it in a par-ticularly caustic way. External criticism like that often makes writers feel dreadful about revising. There are variations of the Fevers: First, what I call Mud Fever is when you get stuck in revision mode. I've met a number of people who've been revising the same memoir or novel for more than ten years, to the detriment of creating any new work. Mud Fever is really a symptom of three different writing viruses, and trying to revise with any of them is using rewriting as an obstacle to your writing rather than in service to it.

Number one, Perfectionism, is the misbegotten belief that, given enough time and information, you can make a piece of writing flaw-less and that only faultless writing is acceptable from the likes of

someone as flawed as yourself. The cure for Perfectionism is to cultivate the perspective of the ancient Greeks, who called the ambition of
perfection hubris and saw it as an arrogance that eventually causes a
person's downfall. The ancient Greeks believed that perfection is the
realm of the gods and that imperfections are a necessary part of
human creation. Ancient Greek artisans actually purposely included
flaws in their creations to avoid the possibility of hubris so the gods
wouldn't punish them for even unintentional arrogance. Of course,
in a very real sense, being caught up in the impossible task of perfecting is its own painful penalty.

The next writing virus, Trying Syndrome, is when you derive a
sense of self-esteem from trying rather than from achieving. A writer
in this state resists finishing projects. She holds on to manuscripts
like a security blanket. Finishing a piece is too scary. It might anger
someone. Some of us feel guilty when we succeed. As a writer, you may
need to address this issue in other areas of your life before your Writing Self can recover from it.

The third virus, Fear of Further Expectations, is when you get
caught up in your own or someone else's expectation that your piece
must be more brilliant and stunning than your last one, or that in
some way what you're writing will prove your worth as a writer. In such
a state of mind, the pressure you or others place upon you makes it
impossible to rewrite. The only cure is to put these impossible expectations aside by reminding yourself that the creative process isn't linear. We all make progress in roundabout ways. Sometimes our worst
writing leads to our best; for example, when we learn from writing a
dull and predictable dialogue between characters what it is that makes
good dialogue exciting.

In addition to these three variations on Mud Fever, there is Judgment Fever, a delirium that arises when your natural ability to evaluate
and analyze swells, causing your inner critic to go on a rampage. As
I've said, the essence of revision is an exercise of intuition, not critical

analysis. Your critical facilities are meant to act as a servant to your intuition, not the other way around. But besides taking the driver's seat away from your intuition, your critical self can become infected with a high level of contemptuousness that paralyzes your revising ability. Your critic is turning disdainful and humiliating when you engage in belittling self-talk as you revise, such as saying to yourself, "How idiotic," or "Jeez, a three-year-old could write a better sentence." Another symptom is if you revise by looking only for what's wrong with your piece instead of also being able to see where to build on what's working and to appreciate what is already well written. When your critical faculties are exacerbated and take up too much space in your psyche, don't rewrite until balance is restored. Otherwise you may end up further exasperating the overblown critic while undermining the strength of your intuition. To restore balance, instead of rewriting, try cooling your Judgment Fever by coaxing your intuition out of the sidelines in whatever ways entice it. Some of the exercises from Percolation, such as cloud watching and daily writing, could help.

Whether you skip rewriting entirely or you need to postpone it until you can approach it positively, the decision not to revise is a valid choice when your reasons are clear.

Practice

∽ PERFECT MISTAKES

Sometimes in writing, as in life, the cure is in the ailment. When the perfectionist virus of Mud Fever arises, you can use an aspect of the virus in a mild form to help recover from it. This is a simple technique with powerful results that challenges perfectionism anytime it comes up while you're rewriting a draft. Do what the ancient Greeks did to guard against hubris: Beginning with a short piece that you're ready to revise, intentionally leave in an imperfection. No matter how strongly you feel about making the imperfection right or better, resist the urge. For a week just live with the imperfection. Read the piece once a day. This is a way to become acclimated to flaws. At first, rereading the draft with an obvious fault may drive you crazy, making it nearly impossible to focus on what you've said in the draft or causing you to practically itch with the impulse to grab a pen or the keypad and fix the defect. After a week's time it should be somewhat easier for you to tolerate the unrefined spot in the draft and appreciate the content and structure of the rest of the piece. Especially early in the week, practice some self-soothing talk if your perfectionist tendency manifests in self-critical chatter. Remind yourself that you aren't your imperfections or that you're apprenticing yourself for the week to the wisdom of the ancient Greeks. When the week is up, you can rewrite your imperfection or let it stand. Don't be surprised if you find that you've actually grown fond of it.

MAKE ROOM FOR NOT REVISING

There is a small subset of writers who are able to toss away all their false starts, half starts, and unrealized pages of writing that didn't add up to a finished piece. They write and revise without the clutter of stray images and unformed ideas from past projects surrounding them. The rest of us are attached to our clutter. We save almost everything we produce just in case it might fit into another writing project or with the idea that we might get back to it later. So many pages or files of unrealized material can burden your revising process unless they are in some sort of order. Too many writers pile all their unfinished drafts in a corner or have them haphazardly tucked away in different places. In the recesses of these writers' minds, they associate revising with their image of these unruly, unfinished drafts.

You can clear your psyche of the clutter and at the same time become clear that revising is a choice you are making by physically creating files. Make three separate files, one for pieces you will not revise, a second for pieces that aren't ready to be revised because of the emotional hold they still have on you, and a third for half starts and false starts.

The key to making this practice work is not to labor over deciding which pieces of writing go into which file. You can always change your mind later and switch something from one category to another. Your goal here is to create order and a sense of choice, not to make hard-and-fast decisions once and for all. Simply skim each piece and ask yourself, Am I basically interested or uninterested in working on this? Does the piece still have an emotional hold on me? Is this something I've begun but don't know how to finish or even if it's worth finishing? Put each piece of writing in its corresponding file along with a complete list of all the pieces in the file.

Once you have sorted your old pieces of writing this way, you can use the files to support unburdened revising. Put aside an afternoon four times a year to review the contents of each of these files to see if there are pieces you have changed your mind about and want to switch into another of the categories or take out and start revising. This practice gives you a manageable way to check in with past drafts, and it gives you more literal and psychic room to decide when and when not to revise.

Eleven

DIRECTED REVISION: WRITING TEACHERS AND CLASSES

When you work with a writing teacher or take a writing class, you are practicing a version of revision in which you're asking others to point out the way. You resee your writing, which is the work of the revision process, through the eyes of teachers and classmates. You take a class or choose a teacher because you're seeking something—new skills, information, affirmation, evaluation, wisdom, a reason to focus on your writing, a new outlook on your work, rejuvenation, community. Also, teachers and classes give your Writing Self an arena in which to develop revising skills out of isolation and in a concerted way.

Like writing expert Jack Hodgins, you may believe that writing classes are useful only until we become our own best editors, but I disagree. Classes and teachers are part of revision work that is done in community. To be nourished as a writer, we need to cycle through stages of learning from others throughout our writing life. Even the most famous writers improve their writing in community through the literature they read, feedback from the editors of their books, and conversations with colleagues. Such encounters influence their writing.

When you enter into a relationship with a teacher or with your colleagues in a class, you are journeying outside your own borders. It's like visiting another country: an adventure of sorts. Like all travelers, when you are away from home your senses are heightened and your preconceived notions are challenged. You are also more vulnerable to what others think about your writing than when tucked away alone at your familiar writing place. So you must enter the arena with your eyes open and with realistic expectations in order to use your relationship with a teacher or classmates in the service of revisioning your writing.

Almost everyone who writes has had at least one experience with a teacher. The benefits are clear and immediate: Just making a commitment of time, money, and energy can improve your focus and concentration. It's invigorating for your Writing Self to be in an apprentice relationship with someone who cares as much about the craft as you do but who is further along in certain insights than you are. From this teacher, you may learn techniques or refine them. But every writing teacher has limitations. Not even the best of us can perform magic by making skills appear or challenges disappear. We can inspire you, enthuse you, inform you, and give you knowledge you need to move ahead. We share our experiences, perspectives, and suggestions. We show you examples. We offer tools for you to experiment with that come from a combination of our own teachers' knowledge, our writing life, and our intuition. Your part in the relationship is to try out our offerings, then keep, toss, or modify them as you see fit.

Writing teachers are *not* authorities on how you should revise or even whether or not you should write. And nothing we can tell you, by itself, should make or break your writing spirit. We influence your Writing Self in the same way that the healing arts impact your body. An acupuncturist can balance your *chi*, but can't keep it balanced if you abuse your body and soul. A chiropractor can adjust your spine, but the adjustment won't hold if you keep moving the same way. Just as such help serves the body but alone won't cure or control it, so writing teachers can serve your Writing Self, but we can't maintain its needs.

That said, all writing teachers are not created equal. Some teachers *are* better than others. For one thing, not everyone who teaches writing is a writing teacher. Some are writers who teach to supplement their income or to earn their living. For another, there is no relationship between a person's talent as a writer and as a teacher. Writing and teaching are two separate forms of communicating. A writer may know a lot about his art. But if he feels resentful about having to teach, or bitter or insecure about his own work, if he doesn't know how to facilitate class-feedback sessions or is too busy writing to attend to his students, he can't impart his knowledge to you in a productive way. For these reasons, it isn't unusual for people who have had several writing teachers to have a negative or disappointing encounter with one or more of them.

When I look back on my share of painful experiences with teachers, I'm amazed I didn't give up on revising or, for that matter, on writing entirely, although I understand why I kept at it. It's related to a concept June Jordan brings up in her collection of essays, *Technical Difficulties*. Jordan contends that self-interest, not democracy, was at the heart of the intentions of the writers of America's Declaration of Independence, but that democracy is such a powerful and right idea that the founding fathers set its evolution in motion just by invoking its name. I believe the same is true of the Writing Self. Once you call it up, it has its own momentum, and although there's plenty that can and will slow it down, there's nothing that can stop it.

I had a teacher who did nothing to discourage fellow class participants from making judgmental, denigrating remarks about one another's writing, including mine. Another teacher offered to give me feedback on my poems and responded only by informing me that until I realized I was going to die I should quit writing poetry. In my early twenties, I was invited to meet a prominent poet and teacher, who had never seen my writing. After fifteen minutes the poet asked me my last name and then told me that with a name like Goldberg, I could forget about being a poet. If I hadn't been such a vulnerable, insecure twenty, I might have been able to laugh at the irony of this award-winning poet of color writing me off because of my ethnic name. But I was devastated. I thought somehow just by looking at me he could see I had nothing to offer. In part, his ability to have such an adverse effect on me was because of my own mistaken belief, or rather my hope that anyone could tell me if I should write, if I was good enough. Without realizing it I was searching in measurements and comparisons for approval and love. I was using my Writing Self to try to gain self-esteem. It didn't work. I was looking for pears from an apple tree.

It would be simpler to say that we can benefit only from working with a talented, loving writing teacher, but that just isn't true. Every teacher is a window into the writing process, especially the rewriting aspect of it, because the ideas a teacher offers are catalysts for rethinking, reseeing, in short, revising not only a piece you're working on but your whole relationship to the writing process. You always have the choice to accept or reject what a teacher offers. Either way, you'll be clarifying and refining your own perspectives. Sometimes you first have to separate the way a teacher delivers her lesson from the lesson itself. At times, it's taken me years to make that separation. In a sense, to gain the most from our teachers we also have to revise our expectations of how we can learn from them by widening our view. Besides teaching us what we want or need to know, a teacher can enlighten us by exemplifying what we don't want to emulate as well. He may voice the deep fears and negative attitudes we harbor and that we must revise before we can fully appreciate and enjoy our writing talents. There is something to gain from almost all teachers—supportive or difficult— as long as we have realistic expectations and we aren't getting hurt in the process.

Masters, Guides, Guardians, Coaches, and Mentors

One way to gain the most from a writing teacher while protecting your Writing Self from unnecessary harm is to think of teachers in categories: Masters, Guides, Guardians, Coaches, and Mentors. Looking at them in this way allows you to adjust your expectations of them. In a sense the distinctions are artificial because one teacher may embody a combination of these attributes. But the categories are useful constructs for considering the various ways a teacher can benefit you and for clarifying what you currently want from a teacher-student relationship.

Each type of teaching has something to offer, and with respect to revising, each one views the purpose of a student's draft differently. Masters are often the hardest teachers to learn from. They're also, at once, the most compelling and the most intimidating. After all, our thinking goes, Why not study with the best? But the best at what? you must ask. Masters have often achieved impressive accolades for their writing. Their books affect millions of people and receive high praise and reward. But attaining a lot of external recognition doesn't necessarily make a person generous, perceptive, supportive, gracious, or fair. A Master is a master because of the dazzling impact of her written words, not because of her uncanny ability to impart essential knowledge of the craft and soul of writing, or because she can explain or even wants to explain her revising process.

Also, fame creates a kind of charisma around people. Combined with a Master's pre-existing magnetism and the awe we bring with us in the presence of someone we admire, there develops a combustible dynamic: Expectations are high and perhaps inflated. If you sign up for a one-day or full-semester class with a Master, arrive open but not exposed. By this I mean, take the class with the confidence that there's something, one thing, that you will leave with that will be useful.

Actively listen for it. But don't enter the arena of a Master's class feeling needy or desperate, because you may leave feeling worse about yourself and your writing than you did when you first walked in.

My most inspiring humanities teacher in college was a Master with a passion for his subject. Class after class he would lecture and gesticulate, conveying information in no perceivable order. But every seventh or eighth sentence he uttered was profound. The assigned texts weren't nearly as fascinating as the professor's interpretations, which dipped into philosophy, ancient history, and modern physics. While I didn't learn from him how to emulate his way of thinking about a topic, I did come away with several new concepts to think about. In those classes I learned how to sift through meadow grass and spot four-leaf clovers.

In a one-day Master writing class I once took, we were invited to send a poem to the teacher ahead of time. Out of some hundred students, about twenty, including me, took this step. During the class, the Master brought out our poems and said he wanted to read about a half dozen of them to give examples of elements of strong poetry. I was hopeful mine was among them. But it wasn't. Fortunately, by that time in my life I was able to keep from making whether or not he read my poem into the one sure test of my worthiness. As a result, I didn't shut myself off during the rest of the session, and I was able to learn a lot from his teachings that day.

Guides are teachers who show us how to navigate the terrain of the written world. They point out the particulars, the nuances, the ins and outs of their genre. A fiction Guide will explain the elements of a short story, provide examples, and show us where in our stories we are and aren't using the standard elements. We follow guides like Dante's Virgil, and we learn from what they point out. Guides have a sense of commitment to their students. They see their responsibility as acclimating us and providing us with an informative and useful tour through the writing and rewriting world. Guides often maintain an emotional distance from their students and their writing, but they give us solid and concrete feedback and suggestions for revising based on time-honored rewriting principles.

Guardians are teachers who put the writing ahead of their students' personalities. In a workshop in which participants comment on one another's writing, Guardians protect their students' drafts from useless criticism. Guardians create an atmosphere with clearly defined parameters to allow students to experiment as they rewrite. The Guardian's goal is to help our writing pieces be the best they can be. Everyone's writing is respected. If we bring a draft to class, the Guardian treats it as a necessary and worthy piece of writing that must be given every opportunity to flourish. A Guardian would never tell us to abandon a piece. These teachers tend not to make global statements about our writing, our style, or the state of the literary arts. They see their role as serving the greater good of the specific pieces of writing we present to them. A Guardian is like a midwife who assists in the birth of our draft in its final form.

Coaches are the teachers who see their job as helping you, the writer, improve your skills. They show you that they're on your side by challenging you to push your Writing Self further. If you don't trust that your Coach believes in your writing, it's hard to embrace her invitations to go deeper or broader in your drafts. A Coach sees her students as being in training and so may also treat your latest draft as practice ground. She might suggest you rewrite your story about a caged lion from the point of view of the cage, for example, to help you stretch your writing capability. She uses what you bring her to do her job of coaxing more from you. Turning your draft into a finished piece isn't her main goal. She wants you to try writing techniques for the sake of encouraging you to explore whatever untapped resources you have.

Mentors are nurturers who encourage our writing, support our efforts, and reflect back to us our own passion and value as writers. We bask in their vision of our work and gain confidence in our words, our intuition, our calling as writers. Mentors focus almost entirely on the positive elements of our drafts. They point out what we can do well and encourage us to do more of it. They cheer us on when we want to try something new. They help us find our audience. Some people sign up for writing class after writing class in search of the Mentor. To acknowledge such an oasis of support or mourn its absence is often necessary before you can write from a place beyond your desire to be the most adored.

Lots of people find their teachers in the form of books. Writing books like this one can provide inspiration and information. Memoirs, collected letters, biographies, and great works of literature can be teachers as well. It's often easier to accept the challenges of a Coach or find the perfect Mentor in the pages of a book. For those who learn best by example, reading well-written novels teaches them what they need to know in order to revise their own novel. Keep in mind, too, that your best writing teachers may not be writing teachers. My acupuncturist, for example, has taught me a lot about my physical energy that I apply to revising my writing.

If you are unable to work with a writing teacher, consider signing up for a short non-writing course with the intention of relating what you learn to your rewriting process. You can apply a teacher's lessons about placement in a flower-arranging class to how you reorganize the plot of your story. You might apply a calligraphy instructor's explanation of the reasons for including various flourishes on your lettering as a strategy to flesh out descriptive sections of your novel. Whatever their discipline, all good teachers in some way help you shift your understanding of rewriting and writing in general for the better; they assist you in revising your approach.

Writing Classes

You increase the benefits of rewriting with input when you take a writing class. Because you're interacting with the other participants as well as the teacher, there's potential for soaking up a wider spectrum of writing and revising insights. Being exposed to how other people rewrite their drafts or even how they approach an assigned writing exercise differently from you gives you new ideas for your own writing. Seeing writing challenges similar to yours in a classmate's draft can help you recognize the problem in your own draft more easily. And your classmates' various opinions about your writing supply you with several rewriting choices, which keeps your concept of revision fluid.

That said, your fellow classmates are just as much of a prospective source of learning or of disappointment as a teacher. On the positive side, you might connect with several like-minded students and maybe even go on to form a writing group together after the class is over. Or you could connect with one other member in particular and later become writing partners. But because each person takes a class for his own reasons, those reasons may not mesh with yours. When you're at odds with a fellow classmate's agenda, don't let the conflict compromise what the class has to offer. Respect your differences and be discerning about how you give that person feedback and how you receive theirs so you don't waste your time arguing with each other.

The members of a class generally include a cross-section of people interested in writing. Some writers thrive on taking classes for just this reason, continually reseeing their writing through the eyes of arbitrary mixes of classmates. Their responses to your writing are tastes of a slice of your potential audience of readers. So, for example, if you're taken aback by a class member's offense at your fictional portrayal of a plumber, rather than feeling frustrated, it's a chance for you to consider whether or not to revise your characterization. And if one student says his goal is to write stories that touch people's hearts and another person's main ambition is to be proud of what he writes, their differing aims prompt you to reflect on your own reasons for writing. Each class session is an occasion to reexamine your writing, which is revising it.

An important consideration in choosing a writing class is your learning style. Do you learn best from regular weekly meetings or intensive day- or week-long sessions? Do you want to learn specific techniques, such as plot and dialogue or how to write compelling mystery, or are you looking for a class that invigorates your writing in general? Are you more productive when you're given writing assignments to complete or when taking part in a workshop format where participants bring in what they already happen to be writing for feedback?

Whatever style of class you take, even if it's within a formal creative writing program, if you don't feel you're getting something valuable from it, get out of the class. While it's good for writers to try techniques or projects that are hard, especially in a supportive atmosphere, there's nothing more harmful to your Writing Self than subjecting it to a diminishing experience such as having your work dismissed or being in a highly competitive situation any longer than necessary. If you feel yourself shriveling up, because you dread going to class or there's not even one member of the group you feel a connection to, or you feel intimidated by the teacher, consider whether you're in the midst of learning a good hard writing lesson or whether it's time to get out. If you end up mistaking a hard class for a bad one, rest assured that the challenge the class raised will resurface again in your writing life until you tackle it. On the other hand, you could be in a class in which the teacher is truly more destructive than constructive, or it may be that for where you are in your writing process the particular style, content, or environment isn't right. Foster your Writing Self's ability to revise by championing its capacity to pick and choose influence and direction from others.

We must keep learning as writers. When we experience teachers, books, or other encounters, we replenish our well of creativity, and as a result we have more to give to our writing. The way we receive input from others is a less literal, more poetic way of revising. It's revisioning. We affirm our writing as a source of learning, we come out of isolation, and as a result we revision: We see our writing with new eyes.

Practice

∼ THE EXORCIST EXERCISE

This is one of the most cleansing exercises I know for preparing to work with a teacher or take a class. I often ask my students to do it at our first meeting. It's hard to show your writing to teachers or class-mates or to get the most from their feedback when you're carrying around painful memories of sharing your writing. There's always a part of your psyche that's hunched up, anxiously awaiting another blow to your Writing Self. Your experience during class is filtered through that worried part of you, skewing your perception of what your teacher or classmate is saying about your writing.

As a way to exorcise any hold bad memories may still have on you, write about a time when someone told you that you weren't a good writer. Think back to a point when events or comments left you feeling diminished as a writer. It may not be an occasion when a person came out and said those words to you; a look, an attitude, the tone of a rejec-tion letter are strong messages, too. Once you have your point in mind, tell the story of what happened. Be as detailed as you like. You could, for example, start by writing about events that led up to the moment. When you're done, be sure your story is on a physical piece of paper.

Now you're ready for the exorcism. At this phase, there's no one right way to drive out the memory. Your goal is to take the sting out of the experience. Choose one of the following methods that resonates for you:

1. Write about another experience in which someone made you feel great about being a writer. Read this story to yourself

aloud three times in a row as a way to deepen its significance in your psyche and thereby lessen the importance of your negative experience.

2. Crumple up your diminishing story into a ball, put it on the floor, and smash it with your foot as hard as you can as a way of physically and symbolically stamping out its power over you. Throw away the flattened memory.

3. Share your hurtful story with a trusted writing friend or artist who will listen empathetically without commenting as a way of diffusing feelings of embarrassment or shame that you associate with the incident.

4. Rewrite your painful story in the third person, as if it happened to someone else, as a way of gaining some emotional distance from it. In your journal, write an empathetic letter to that someone else consoling him or her. Read the letter aloud to yourself twice and hear it as a letter from you to your Writing Self.

∽ INSTRUCTOR INVENTORY

It's never too late to learn from a teacher. To make the most of your writing teachers, list past and present ones and what you learned from each. Classify each teacher in terms of being a Master, Guide, Guardian, Coach, or Mentor (see page 121). You can make up combinations if you need to. For instance, a teacher could be 70 percent Coach and 30 percent Mentor. Now that you have each one pegged, so to speak, is there something new you can glean from your experiences with them? Now that you see that your last fiction teacher was a Guide, for instance, are you able to put aside your idea that she thought you were only a fair writer because she didn't connect with you more personally? Can you now look back at the general advice she gave the class and use it with the same enthusiasm as if it were given to you specifically? You can also use the inventory to determine the type of support you currently want from a teacher, by noticing which type of teaching taught you the most or which category of teacher you haven't experienced yet.

Twelve

COMMUNAL REVISION: WRITING GROUPS AND PARTNERS

Working with a writing group or a writing partner is another apsect of revising, because it influences how you see your writing. Groups and partners are your immediate, regular writing community. They are the people you personally choose to share the revising process with in an ongoing and formal way. Friends and family who read and respond to your writing are not a substitute. Some writing groups exist for the purpose of making time to write during the meeting, which isn't strictly the work of revision, but is still a good reason to join with other writers and encourage one another. Since most groups form to support work that members have already begun, they concern themselves primarily with rewriting.

Writing Groups

A writing group is a sanctuary. At a regular, appointed time, you gather with kindred spirits, fellow devotees of language, to attend to the written word. Your group is your first audience, your deep listeners, and sometimes even the purveyors of uninterrupted time for you to write. All the members care about the written world in a way that compels them to write. All of them have put as much trust in you to treat their work respectfully as you've put in them. Even if you have different goals—publication, a commitment to write, a need for a writers' community—and your views on writing vary, group members show up for one another, whether or not they have any of their own writing to share.

Your responsibilities are different in a writing group than in a writing class. In a class, a teacher sets the tone, structure, and content for the course, and it's her job to maintain the environment she establishes. Her evaluation of your writing is the most significant; her teachings influence your classmates' feedback on your work.

In a writing group, you haven't come together arbitrarily in a classroom. You've chosen one another. Everyone starts out on equal footing with his and her own ambitions. You enter into a covenant of sorts with the other members: You agree to be close readers of one another's writing, to be helpful and supportive to the best of your abilities, and to show up at every meeting. The commitment members make to the group is an affirmation of each person's Writing Self.

When you bring a piece of writing to the group, you practice a unique aspect of revision. Your writing group becomes an extension of the laboratory of your desk. Your commitment to the group affords you an attentive audience that honestly tells you the impressions your writing makes. Over time, the members of a writing group develop a history with one another's work. They have the additional perspective to see a story you bring to the group in the context of past stories you've written. You aren't revising in isolation. You accept influence instead of protecting yourself from it.

Communal revision establishes a place to process your writing with your guard down. It's a detrimental modern myth that writers do their work all alone. There are stages when it's just us and our words, and stages when we gain more by inviting others into the process. This is the communal aspect of writing that is so often lacking in writers' lives. The absence of this community deprives the Writing Self of essential resources. Meeting with fellow writers at a café to toss around ideas and theories is inspiring, but it won't replace the bone closeness of joining with fellow writers to attend to one another's writing. You expose a piece that's still in formation, and the group members reveal how it makes them think and feel: You show them yours, they show you theirs. If this sounds a bit like lovemaking it's because communal revision is an equally intimate process, one the Writing Self desires almost as much as people desire sex. After all, writing, like making love, is a form of communication, and revision is a facet of the writing process that requires trust and vulnerability in order to cultivate the most complete level of understanding. When we seek out one another and gather into groups or partnerships, we fulfill one of our most essential writing and revising roles by formally attending to the nuances of the written word together.

Pyramids, Constellations, Webs

Writing groups disappoint us writers when group dynamics prevent them from providing an intimate writing connection. Groups offer support only when they function like a web, with members interconnected and interdependent. In a web, each strand or group member is necessary and valued. The web, or the group's strength, depends on all the strands relying on one another equally. When people become disenchanted with their group it's often because it has shifted in shape from a web to a pyramid or a constellation.

Pyramids form when the group believes that certain members offer better feedback—usually those who are writing teachers or published authors. In a pyramid, the group settles into an unspoken hierarchy, and members find themselves discounting one person's feedback, hearing another one's as gospel, and feeling like their own comments are mediocre.

Constellations emerge when mini-groups or subsets form within a group: all the men, for example, all the essayists, all those who knew each other before the group formed. Members start feeling obliged to censor their comments out of loyalty to their constellation, or they discount the comments of those outside their constellation. Alternatively, people may feel that a particular constellation doesn't give equal attention to the work of those outside of it. It's normal for writing groups or individual members of a group to go through periods of discord and then harmonize on their own. Such stages are like the temporary obstacles we encounter when we revise our work alone at home. But when your group gets stuck in an unproductive dynamic, you have to take steps to reestablish the shape. Productive writing groups often include a yearly or quarterly meeting in which everyone can air concerns and make suggestions. The discussion gives each member a chance to notice, appreciate, and be active in how the group is evolving.

To maintain the web shape of your writing group so it helps everyone revise, five members of long-standing writing groups offer their wisdom:

1. Have goals

When you give group members a draft to look at, ask them for feedback in a specific area. A starting place for members to respond makes everyone feel focused and productive. Do you want to know if the dialogue is realistic? Or whether your material would make a better short story or magazine piece than a novel? Ask. You can ask that your group say nothing and just listen to your new story or that they tell you only what they love about it.

Periodically, everyone should articulate the writing goal that motivates them to participate in the group; for example, to push a current comfort zone, to get inspired by the work of others, to get help with rewriting. If anyone's goal has changed—at first a member wanted help with narrative drive but now he wants the group's support in trying to write in a new genre—this periodic check-in helps the group reorient their feedback.

But it doesn't matter if your goal differs from the help you actually receive in the group, as long as you feel you're getting something useful out of the meetings.

2. Feedback

A writing group spends most work sessions giving and receiving feedback on members' work. The idea is for everyone to learn something through the discussion, of each piece.

If you start zoning out when someone else's story is up for discussion, you lose out. One way to stay focused is to listen for how the comments could apply to rewriting your own draft.

Giving feedback to others is a revision exercise. In responding to someone else's work, you're practicing the skills you use to revise—you choose the words and approach that speak most convincingly to your audience.

Before you respond to a group member's draft, ask yourself, How can I help? Is what helps me the same as what will help this person? That way, you will have a place from which to begin your response, and you won't offer an apple to a person without any teeth. You'll serve up applesauce instead.

3. Comparisons

Whenever you present your writing along with other people's, you create the potential to compare your work. At moments you may feel jealous, inferior, arrogant, or judgmental. You're naturally prone to the feelings you experience in other areas of your life.

I was once part of a group in which I felt inferior to the other members. I considered dropping out. It was hard to feel that my writing was the weakest in the group, and I wished that the comments members made were given more sensitively. But the feedback I was getting was valuable. I decided that I could stay in the group if I either asked people to give their suggestions in a more considerate way or joined a second group with a gentler atmosphere as a way of providing balance for myself. Rather than avoid the comparison I was making, or toughing it out, or waiting for my comparing tendency to disappear, I treated my feelings like the revising blocks I have at my desk. I found a way to work with them.

Writing Partners

Instead of joining a writing group, some people connect with just one other writer and establish a writing partnership with that person. Partnering can include several types of exchanges. The two of you might swap drafts for feedback and support. You could be collaborating on a book project or an article. Each of you might serve as the check-in person for the other as you complete writing goals such as finishing a chapter, revising a poem, writing a query letter, or trying a new genre.

I once partnered with another writer for the purpose of submitting poems to magazines. We each tended to procrastinate about making our work public, and one day, when we were bemoaning the fact that we couldn't afford to hire assistants to do it for us, we decided to become each other's assistant. We divided up about twenty literary journals and each asked our half for submission guidelines. We pooled our information, gave each other a stack of our poems, and each selected poems and wrote cover letters for the other. We kept track of which of our partner's poems were where and what the results were, and we let our partner know when a poem was accepted and spared her from having to read rejection letters. Our partnership in publication made the whole process of submission almost fun.

The most significant difference between writing partnerships and writing groups is the depth of relationship. A group is like an extended family; a partnership is more like a marriage. Instead of opening yourself to several other writers at once, you focus your whole commitment on your partner, and she does the same for you. The intensity of coupling this way can feel deeply nurturing. Like a strong marriage, your talents balance each other. My friend Brandel just completed a book with her writing partner. She finds the relationship invaluable. "I am capable of going into image-overload. I start pumping out metaphors and images at an alarming rate, and she helps pare down my sentences so that the beauty of a single image can shine."

It's also simpler to negotiate changes in purpose or meeting times with only one other person. You can keep up the relationship even while living a great distance apart. But partnerships also have the potential to bring up the darker aspects of your psyche in a concentrated form, such as a strong competitive or jealous streak. Only you can gauge how well you and your partner would deal with some of the same situations that turn writing groups from webs into pyramids. How would you handle it if one of you was more prolific than the other or received more recognition or success with publication? Writing groups and partners nourish your revising process only when they support your work, your respect for your Writing Self, and your sense of place and community in the written world.

Practice

✑ TAKE YOUR TEMPERATURE

If you're part of a writing group or you're considering joining one, make a list of what you hope to gain. Be honest with yourself. Write down whatever comes up even if it's unrealistic. You don't have to show it to anyone. The list is your thermometer. It marks your expectations and your progress. Review it occasionally. Are you getting what you want from the group? Have your goals changed? If so, tell your group. Once a member of my writing group announced that she no longer wanted the group to be the only place where she shared her writing. We helped her find venues by bringing in fliers about open readings and calls for anthology submissions. "Is this story one you're considering sharing outside of the group?" we asked before discussing it. If the answer was yes, we incorporated her new goal into the feedback we gave her on the draft. In turn, she felt the support in going public that she needed to stick with it.

If your writing group isn't meeting your expectations, make a second list of anything that you are gaining from the experience. If you can't think of one positive and worthwhile gain, try the next exercise. If that doesn't help, skip your next meeting and use the time to reflect. Is it time for you to move on and leave the group? Can you return to the group and ask for something that you want, something that you think the group can supply, such as opinions about which sections of your draft are working or time for you to hear a portion of your draft read aloud by another member? Revisit your writing group at least once before completely dropping out, both to be absolutely sure it's what you want to do and to be respectful by formally saying good-bye.

∾ PRACTICE WHAT YOU PREACH

The spiritual precept that when you help others you help yourself especially applies in writing groups. But only if you pay attention to the help you are giving and apply it to your own writing. In life, time and again, the counsel I give a friend, whether about a relationship, a career move, or anything else, turns out to be advice I myself need to follow. When I get ready to offer my opinion to a friend, a part of me says to myself, "Watch what you say!" But of course I don't. I can't, because I need to hear it, too. It's taken me a long time to acknowledge the relationship between what I say and what I need to hear in my writing group. I can be pretty resistant about learning as a writer. Here's how I broke through my resistance and how you can, too.

If you're already part of a writing group, the next time you meet, take notes on what you and the other members say about everyone else's draft instead of noting only what people say about your own piece. Read over these notes before each of your next three rewriting sessions and look for comments you or the group made about other members' writing that are sound advice for your own piece. Take the advice.

Thirteen

REVISING
OBSTACLES

Now that you have a set of revising tools to work with, the next step is to use them wisely. Although there are writers who can revise their first draft as they write it, you will often deal more effectively with revising concerns after you finish an initial draft. That doesn't mean that you don't rewrite an occasional sentence or paragraph as you set your first draft down or that you shouldn't reread your last chapter and make a few changes before moving on to the next chapter. But if you revise every word as you write it, you put yourself at risk of being so caught up in adjusting what you just put down that you write yourself into circles, become totally frustrated, and abandon the initial draft altogether.

As you write a first draft, questions arise such as how to begin the piece or how to connect all the ideas, scenes, and events, which you can't resolve until you complete the draft. I've known plenty of writers who struggle with finishing their first drafts because they keep trying to use revision to address these questions. A body analogy for this revision-first draft relationship is when you pinch a nerve in your back, but you experience the pain in your leg. No matter what you do to your aching leg, it won't stop hurting until the nerve is attended to. Similarly, sometimes your first-draft problem is relieved only by alleviating the pressure to revise it before you're done.

On the other hand, you *will* have to draw on parts of your revising *experience* to help you write your draft through to the end. You know, for example, that your main character has to recover a lost memory early in his story. You decide to write it as a dream. Halfway through, you start to wonder if it wouldn't work better for him to have the memory during an encounter with someone. Later, you come up with a third possibility, that his memory surfaces while he's reading a newspaper article. If you stop writing the rest of the story until you've rewritten the scene all three ways and chosen among them, and you continue to work on the story this way, you could, potentially, never finish it. But if you draw on your past revising experience—that as your understanding of a character deepens you have a clearer sense of how he comes to epiphanies—you can postpone your decision. Make a note to yourself in the margin—dream, encounter, or newspaper article—and come back to it when the first draft is done. What you know from your past revision experience helps you complete the draft.

The obstacle to using what you already know about revision to finish a first draft is usually insufficient revision experience to draw from. Three revising obstacles that show up when you try to write a first draft are worth exploring to see if any of them point to an area of revision that you may need to further develop:

Do You Have Too Many Ideas?

At the first-draft stage, some people feel so overwhelmed by ideas that they find it impossible to take hold of a single topic without all the others interfering with their concentration. Maybe you think you'd love too many ideas to be your problem, but trust me, it can be as paralyzing as not having any ideas at all. Too many ideas can seriously clog up the works.

Part of rewriting is linking one idea to another; for instance, connecting the conversation between best friends on page three to the scene with them on the beach on page twenty-three. The relationship between the conversation and what takes place on the beach may not seem obvious at first, but because you have experience with revising, you know that as you reread, pare down, embellish, and rearrange your words, the connection will become clear. When you write a first draft and you get flooded with thoughts, your experience with how ideas connect during rewriting helps you keep writing. You trust that the relationships between your ideas will become clearer to you over time. As a result, you're able to allow all your thoughts, no matter how seemingly disparate, to pour out in words in the first draft. You understand that the connections are there without having to see them immediately.

Do You Lose Your Momentum?

Another first-draft problem that requires your revision experience is when you run out of steam mid-draft. You have an idea that excites you. You start writing, but suddenly you can't think of anything else to say; you feel as if you've written yourself up against a wall. When you can't complete a first draft, it's often for one of the same reasons it can be difficult to revise: Your intuition has lost control of the process and your intellect has taken charge. Your logical and critical side looks at your half-finished first draft and sees only disorder, chaos, and missing pieces. No more writing until you clean up the mess, it tells you. And you listen.

If you can't keep up the momentum of your idea through a whole draft, jump-start your intuitive faculties. Put your draft aside and journal for a while on a totally different subject to give your intuition a fresh place to resurface. Or randomly read three or four past entries in your journal. It will help you reconnect to the free-flowing aspect of your mind that journaling encourages, and in the process you might find a passage you once wrote that relates to your draft. I also find that rereading favorite books eases me back into a creative-intuitive state and renews my motivation to write.

ARE YOU CONFUSED ABOUT HOW TO BEGIN YOUR DRAFT?

If your obstacle is that you can't begin your draft at all, you've confused the decision about how your piece will open with getting started on writing it. Where your piece begins is a question to consider when you're ready to revise, not when you start writing a first draft. If you're writing about your divorce, for example, you don't have to first figure out when the trouble in your marriage began and start writing there. You could write out a typical argument between you and your ex, describe your honeymoon, or inventory all the ways you rearranged your house after your spouse moved out. To get started on a piece, begin writing absolutely any part that you can. Then later, after you get your first draft done, during revision, decide which passage is the best one to open the piece. There isn't a specific place or a specific way to begin any piece of writing. Instead, there are countless entry points, and every one is an equally good way to start writing.

The solutions to these particular first-draft obstacles come out of developing your revising experience. But when you've completed the first draft and it's time to use all of your revising skills, there's one obstacle that all of us face before we can rewrite: emotion.

Disappointment, Fear, and Love

It's common to read over a first draft and react in three ways. You think it's garbage, you fall completely in love with what you wrote, or you recognize the strong and the problematic sections. As long as you make your way through the others to the third attitude, you can revise.

The typical first reaction is to think your draft is trash, and this usually happens because the words you wrote don't measure up to the grandness of your idea. Disappointment, even disgust, is a normal reaction. You're discouraged because the writing is flat, awkward, or seems hopelessly disorganized. At this stage, without the heart to continue, you can't move past these feelings and revise. You till the soil without planting the garden.

The best way to find your way back into a draft that disappoints you is to get some distance from it. During the week or month you take away from rewriting the draft, remind yourself, in writing, why you wrote the piece in the first place. Was it to help someone else, to preserve an important moment, to help you articulate an idea that matters a great deal to you? With your renewed sense of purpose, go back to the draft and find one place—a phrase, a sentence, a short passage you feel good about—and start rewriting from just before or just after that point. If there isn't any part of the piece you like, bring it to your writing group. Now is the time to ask the members to read your draft and comment only on what is wonderful about it.

The next hurdle is the fear that you can't do it: can't make the writing clear, can't articulate your ideas more simply, can't find the right structure. Your fear is also quite a normal part of revising. It's when you allow your fear to stop you from revising that it becomes threatening. Otherwise, fear is a good indication that your writing is nourishing you by providing you with real challenges that will stretch your Writing Self. There is a legitimate reason to feel afraid. Most of the work you revise will confront you with an aspect of writing, that you haven't mastered. In a long and productive life of writing you will be confronted many times with such challenges. They are part of the point of rewriting—to push you beyond your current limits. Your best tool for overcoming your fear is your commitment to revise in spite of your fear.

When I write poems, I have an opposite reaction to a draft. I'm more apt to fall head over heels in love with my first draft than to hate it or worry over how to improve it. I was embarrassed the first time I admitted this in my writing group. Once I've fallen in love, it's nearly impossible for me to revise until my passion has cooled. Some writers are monogamous this way; as soon as they write the next piece and fall in love with it, they can revise the older piece. Not me. There's no telling when the love affair will turn from eros into agape. Sometimes it takes years. I've learned to be patient and revel in my infatuation. Over the years, I've come to see that eventually I gain the distance to rewrite. I no longer worry that it's egotistical of me to adore my words, either. I trust that as long as they cast a spell over me, they're doing me some good.

Practice

∿ IDEA OVERLOAD

When you get flooded with ideas before you start a first draft, you need the writer's equivalent of a surge protector. You don't want to block the many thoughts and images your imagination is sending you, but you do want to direct their flow so they don't overwhelm your ability to write. Write each image or idea on a small piece of paper, using a single word or phrase. Put all the papers in an envelope or hat. Without looking, pick one out and begin with whichever idea or image you drew. If you pick one and wish it had been another, start writing about the one you had hoped to get. If you get one and feel disappointed with it, pick again up to three times. If you're disappointed by all of them, begin with the first or last one you chose. When you finish writing about the first idea you settled on, draw another one to write about. As you write about the second idea, look for ways it relates to the first idea. But don't be concerned if you see no relationship at all. Just keep drawing topics and writing about them until you've run through them all.

This method isn't as arbitrary as it might appear. You are temporarily short-circuiting what has become, for you, an overdeveloped concern with seeing the big picture of how your ideas are related so that you can accomplish the little-picture work of putting all your ideas into written form. As you use random control to impose order, connections between certain ideas will occur to you. Make only the briefest notations of them in the margins—"vessel image relates to paragraphs three and six"—and keep on drawing ideas and writing about them. The temptation is to go into revision mode and start organizing the connections you already see. But if you give in to this urge, it's likely that you'll approach the ideas you haven't written about yet with the expectation that they must fit neatly into what you've already started revising. You'll find yourself bogged down again by your big-picture perspective.

REVERSALS OF FORTUNE

Whenever you are stuck in the midst of a first draft or a revision, start writing about the opposite of your idea on a separate piece of paper. If you're stumped about how your confident main character handles the news that her husband wants to quit his job and move to a Quonset hut in Belize, write a couple of paragraphs describing her reaction as if she were anxious and paranoid instead. If you're writing an essay that's pro campaign-finance reform, write a short rebuttal to the points you've already made. It's reverse psychology. It's also Newton's law that for every action there's an opposite and equal reaction. You get reinspired from writing about the opposite of your goal.

∽ CROSSROADS COME AND GO

When how to start a draft stops you from ever writing it, you are being waylaid by a revising concern before you have even written anything that can be revised. All roads lead to a completed first draft as long as you travel the road by starting to write. Some people need to peek down each road before they choose. Here's a quick way to satisfy that need and get on to writing. Write down a dozen different possible opening sentences or three separate opening paragraphs. From this exercise one of the openings will stand out as the most appealing and you can follow it. If not, close your eyes and choose one of your beginnings to start from. However resistant you feel about the one you chose, start writing anyway and remind yourself that you can change the opening later. You can even reward yourself with deleting the opening you started with when you've completed a certain number of pages or chapters of your first draft. Keep a copy of the openings you wrote for this exercise but didn't use. Refer back to it when you revise. The list is a record of your first thoughts about the possible directions the piece could go in for you to consult as you make revising decisions.

∽ SECOND THAT EMOTION

Once you've completed a first draft, it becomes subject to all the emotions it took for you to write it. Sometimes you read it over and experience your range of emotions in rapid succession. With your initial emotions out of your system, you're ready to take a few steps back from your draft for the sake of revising it. Other times, you get snagged in one emotion, usually disappointment in the draft or love for each and every word exactly as it appears. Putting the draft away for a few days, weeks, or months gives your emotions time to ease to the point where you can return to your draft with some objectivity. But when time doesn't alleviate the hold your emotions have on your writing, you have to address what is, for you, an overly critical or overly protective tendency. What I'm about to suggest may seem corny or ridiculous. But believe me, it's just the medicine your tendency needs. Write yourself a long, gushing thank-you note about how much you appreciate yourself for taking the time to write the first draft, why the idea is important and powerful to write about, and how future drafts are going to offer even greater insights to you and others. You have to include all three of the above subjects in your letter for it to work. Read it aloud to yourself twice. In Yiddish it's called schmoozing your critical or protective tendency. You're buttering it up so it will relax its grip on your draft. You're approaching your tendency like you'd approach the protective mother who doesn't want her son to travel to the spelling bee championship in a faraway city; by telling her how important her son is, how he'll be the hero of the neighborhood, she sends him off with her blessing.

Fourteen

IS IT FINISHED YET?

How do you know when you're finished revising? There is no single answer. It depends on your definition of finished. Personally, I think of a finished piece as weaned. The original definition of wean was to ripen. When a fruit is ripe it no longer stays attached to the tree. Just like a ripe pear, a finished piece of writing is ready to be food for others and to seed their imaginations. And like a fruit, when a piece of writing is complete it no longer needs to be attached to the writer or to depend on her to communicate to others.

But unlike a tree's fruit, your writings don't automatically grow until they naturally fall away from you. As a writer you're more like the nursing mother: At a certain point you decide it's time to stop. There are some pieces you must nurse longer than others. The length of time it takes to fully dramatize an ethical question in one story, for example, doesn't necessarily equal the time it takes to set the landscape of an historical era in a different story. And just like when weaning a child, you often have mixed feelings of relief and loss when you decide a piece of writing is finished, especially a long one. You might question your timing the way some mothers do about weaning; if only I'd waited a little longer, stopped a little sooner . . . But your overall sense is that the piece is ready to stand on its own.

The word "finished" defines a wide range of ideas, including ended, played out, fulfilled, realized, achieved, resolved, terminated, concluded, perfected, consummated, polished, masterful, skilled, and even the opposites of these notions: ruined, condemned, gone. Because of all these perspectives, one person feels done with a story she's written when it's polished, that is, the language and imagery are refined. Another person is finished when all the aspects of plot and characterization are played out, i.e., when the story makes total sense. Someone else stops writing when the story has gone out of him—right after he's transferred it from his thoughts into written words.

If you write in more than one genre you probably have different criteria for what finished means in each of them. For me, the process of finishing a poem can take a year. I can finish a poem only when it has finished affecting my emotional life. After I bring a draft of a poem to my writing group, I have to put the physical poem away and let it continue to work on my interior world. Months later, I reread the poem to gauge whether I now have enough distance to work on it. When I'm finally capable of making the revisions necessary for it to communicate to others, it's still not finished until I read it aloud to an audience. In the genre of poetry, it is only then that I hear the poem completely independent of my personal relationship to it and therefore hear the final changes I need to make to finish it. I've heard that Robert Frost kept copies of his poems in a locked vault and continued to revise them for years after they were published.

When I write essays and narratives, on the other hand, what I learn or understand from the piece surfaces as I write and revise, usually over a period of a couple of weeks or months. As a result, I finish essays and narratives shortly after I get feedback from others, or soon after I put the piece away for a few weeks and come back to it. The piece is done before it's ever public. As soon as I can read it aloud to myself without faltering over an awkwardly written passage or an unclear idea, and there is a rhythm to the writing, I'm finished.

My book-length pieces of writing are finished when their deadlines are up. Some deadlines are imposed by contracts. Others I make for myself, such as, until the end of the summer or before my birthday. I find it impossible to work on a large scale without these limits. Whether for a first draft or a final one, the deadlines are arbitrary in terms of subject matter or genre. I create deadlines to fit inside the reality of my life's schedule. I find such limits reassuring because the Stickler in me feels secure that there's a goal to work toward and the protests from my Rebel self motivate me to set up a flexible timetable. But deadlines don't work for me with poetry. The pressure of a due date impinges on my creativity.

However you define "finished," the fact is that, like Robert Frost, you can always go back to a piece you've written and find something to fix, because you're not the same writer who originally decided it was done. Writing it changed you: You learned something about writing or you gathered your thoughts or you gained some insight. To keep from becoming an obsessive, Frostian reviser, look at your finished writings as a photo album of the life of your Writing Self. Just as when you look back at old photos you smile at your hairstyles and clothing, reminisce about a certain place or friend, notice your face changing, your children growing, so you can look at your finished pieces of writing. You see the imperfections, the growth; you remember the mistakes you hope you've learned from. Then you turn the page, close the book, and capture another moment in words.

There are many writers and artists who believe that a creative piece is never truly finished. Instead, they view the products of their lifelong creative process as points on a time line that simply mark where they are in their evolution as artists at a particular moment. From this perspective, going public with your writing—the subject of the next and final section—is the part of your process that prepares you for the next cycle of creation. By putting your writing out into the world at certain intervals, you are letting it go, emptying yourself of it so that you are left with only what writing the piece taught you, and so, both lightened and enlightened, you continue on the creative journey. If you define "finished" in this way, your relationship to writing is more focused on the process than it is on the results. Being finished becomes a matter of being ready to move on to the next project because you've grown as much as you can from the last one.

As readers, our window into an author's process is her output. When you fall in love with an author, you're no longer reading only for plot and characters or the style or voice. You read to immerse yourself in the writer's vision of the world. Reading her writing is a means of connecting to her creative approach. The more the pieces you write excite you at each stage of their coming into being—percolation, revision, and going public—the more your relationship with your own creative process is like the one you have with the work of the authors you love and admire. It's really okay to love and admire your own writing process. Then being finished with a story isn't the whole reason for writing it. The pressure to be done in order to feel satisfied is off. You have the freedom to define "finished" as whatever resonates for your creative process.

Practice

⌘ THE FINISH LINE

Measuring your draft against your definition of "finished" is an especially helpful tool for deciding when a piece you're writing is done. To bring your sense of finished to the forefront of your thinking, journal about what finished means to you. If that sounds difficult, you don't have to start your exploration with the subject of writing. For instance, first you can journal about what it means to be finished with your daily workout. Is it when you've had a certain amount of aerobic exercise? When your cooldown is over? When you're dressed and out the door? Or what does it mean to you to be finished cleaning your kitchen? Is it when the dishes are all washed, or when they're put away? Next, try journaling about something that's a bit more open-ended, such as what it means to be finished with a relationship. Finally, write about what your standards for finished are when it comes to your writing.

Another way to approach this exercise is to look back at the list of synonyms for finished on p. 148 and pick out three that interest you. Journal for a couple of paragraphs about each synonym. Read what you've written and see if any of it applies to how you gauge when a piece you're writing is done. If you write in more than one genre, you can also use this journaling exercise to write about what finished means to you in each one. You'll know you're finished with this exercise when you have a clearer idea of what finished means to you. For some people, it is helpful to write out their criteria for being finished on an index card that they can refer to as they work through the final drafts of a piece of writing.

∿ LOVE AND ADMIRATION: THE ALBUM

When you love and admire your writing process and the gifts it gives you, being finished with a piece of writing becomes one integral part of the creative cycle instead of the ultimate goal that all the rest of the writing work you've done leads up to. If I only wrote books so that I could hold the finished product in my hands, I would hate writing.

By the time I'm done writing a book, I'm filled with all that I've learned in the course of writing it, and I'm exhausted by the writing challenges I've had to meet to get it done. The manuscript itself is an emblem or a souvenir of the creative process. It stands for what I've accomplished. Without this deeply nourishing perspective, the day-to-day work of writing loses its juice, and revising a draft becomes merely a means to an end.

You should love your own writing life at least as much as you love the writing of your favorite authors. To cultivate this relationship with your writing, look back at three to five pieces you've finished as if they were photos in an album. You may want to warm up by looking at a real photo album before you do this exercise with writing: Remember who you were when you wrote each piece, how you've changed since then, and one thing you learned about writing since you moved on from each piece. Record these insights in your journal.

For example, when I wrote *Room to Write* I was searching for other ways to share my ideas about the creative spirit besides teaching classes about it. Since writing that book, I've changed by becoming more willing to face my writing challenges. One thing I learned about writing is that when I express myself in written words, I make myself ready for new insights.

By acknowledging the ways you grow as a writer from piece to piece, you support a balanced appreciation for your whole Writing Self.

III

GOING PUBLIC

*Creativity is the link between our inner work
and the outer work that society requires of us.
Creativity is the threshold . . . to actions
of beautification, celebration,
and healing in the world.*

MATTHEW FOX

Fifteen

GO PUBLIC

*His [the writer's] function is to make his imagination theirs [the readers']
and he fulfills himself only as he sees his imagination become the light in the
mind of others. His role, in short, is to help people live their lives.*
WALLACE STEVENS

*Because your existence in time and space is unique,
there are lives that only you can touch.*
HARRY PALMER

The public aspect of writing is the third and final practice you
must take part in to nourish your Writing Self. You may
think of going public as a writer as publishing, but it's much
larger than that. When you make writing, you enter a new relationship
to the written word that includes passing it on to others. Going public
is doing your part to bring the written word to the rest of the world.
The words you offer can be your own or someone else's. You can give
them to a large group of strangers or to a few people you are close to.
But to fulfill yourself and your role as a writer, you must complete the
writing cycle by being public somehow.

We get convoluted messages about going public that are tangled
up in perceptions about publishing companies and best-seller lists
because we don't talk enough about the bigger picture. Writers often

can't see past the publish-with-a-New-York-publisher-or-perish perspective because the value of other options—sometimes even the options themselves—aren't clear. Indifferent agents, editors, and publishers aren't what frustrate your attempts to go public. Your frustration is caused by a set of internal limitations that may include your particular definition of success as a writer, misconceptions about the purpose of going public, a fear of rejection, and misunderstanding your role as a writer. We'll deal with these frustrations and others throughout this section, beginning here by reviving the idea of "sharing," an overlooked definition of going public.

When I use the word "share" to describe the process of making writing public, I'm not trying to be sweet or gentle. Sharing includes neglected aspects of what we writers do when we go public, aspects that keep our relationship to our writing intact. In print or in person, sharing means that you lend your writing to others, give them a turn with it. Whether those people are editors, friends, or an audience of strangers at an open reading, you hope to get your writing back in good shape—without a rejection letter, an indifferent nod, or boos from the audience. But lending anything to anyone is always a risk. If it's your car you lend, it can come back to you dented or with curly fries wedged in the seat cushions. If it's your short story you're sharing, it can come back to you unappreciated. To be nourished by sharing writing, you must accept the risks. Your main reason for sharing can't be to receive other people's praise.

How do you achieve this enlightened perspective? One way is not to share your own writing. You can do your sharing in the world by going public with another writer's work if you're too sensitive to people's reactions to your own. Send an essay about healing to a grieving friend. Go to an open reading and introduce the audience to a favorite poet of yours by reading a few of her poems. These are legitimate ways to share. Poets often begin their readings with a poem written by another poet who inspires them.

But you can also learn how to share your own writing while keeping your relationship to it intact. Think of sharing your writing as similar to offering the triple chocolate mousse cake you baked to a friend. If he doesn't love it, does it ruin your pleasure in baking? Maybe you try the recipe again and work on improving it. Or maybe you give up on that recipe and try another. But if you like baking, you don't abandon doing it when it turns out that you're not the next Betty Crocker. You concentrate your efforts on cookies, or you partner up with a person who has some of the technical know-how you lack. You find your own way to do what you love. It's the same with sharing writing. You can't allow rejection and disappointment to stop you from fulfilling your public role as a writer.

The big difference between sharing your writing and sharing in other parts of your life is that the person with whom you share your writing isn't always someone who personally asked you for a turn. Writers often offer their work unsolicited. For example, you post a copy of your meditation on the nature of reality on the Internet. You might get kudos, suggestions, criticism, or you might be completely ignored, depending upon who notices your piece. The same is true when you send your manuscript to an agent or an editor. Uncertainty and vulnerability are always part of the equation, and going public can feel like giving a piece of your soul away every time you show your writing to others. No wonder so many people either give up on sharing or keep at it feeling resentful and unhappy about their work.

Good Reasons to Share

But there is satisfaction to be gained from sharing writing that nobody can take away from you. To experience it, you must honestly examine your reasons for going public. There are many excellent ones, all of which have to do with love. These reasons enrich your Writing Self, respect you, and respect your audience:

1. *Share in return for the gift of being able to write.* There is a certain responsibility that comes with receiving gifts. When you accept a gift but not the accompanying responsibility, you diminish the gift for yourself, for the giver, and for all those who also might benefit from your having it. Like the gorgeous scarf your beloved gave you that sits in a drawer unworn because you're waiting for the perfect occasion, no one, not yourself, your beloved, nor your friends, ever *receives* the pleasure of seeing you in it. From this perspective, sharing is your part as a writer in building community. You engage people in the imaginative part of their minds to enter the world or idea you create in words. Since it is through our imagination that we experience compassion for others, the connection with others that your words engender makes for a stronger community. In this capacity your ability to write doesn't belong only to you. It's an aspect of Creation you tap into or an aspect that's tapped into you for the sake of a larger purpose.

2. *Share your writing to make room for more.* There's a story about a holy man accompanying his disciples to visit a neighboring temple. When he tries to enter the temple, a force prevents him from being able to grasp the door handle. His concerned disciples ask him what's happening, and he replies, "The temple is too full of prayers for me to enter." Confused, his students ask, "Isn't a temple supposed to be full of prayer?" "No," he says. "The prayers are meant to soar to the Creator on the wings of our intentions. The prayers here aren't sincere. They can't soar, and so they crowd me out." For some people, not sharing writing amounts to the same as praying without authentic intention. Their Writing Self gets clogged up, and there's no room for new writing to enter. On another level, to have a sharing deadline helps you get a piece finished so you can move on to the next one.

3. *Share so that you have no regrets.* For some people, depriving themselves the experience of going public will nag at them for the rest of

their lives. That's why I studied dance and choreography. I simply had to try dancing. I loved it. I went on to teach dance, join a local dance troupe, and choreograph for them and another company. Then I stopped dancing professionally. I was insecure about my technical abilities and a little afraid of the gypsy-like life of dancers waiting tables in between tours and rehearsals. I couldn't take the next step of committing to a dancing career. I regret that, but not nearly as much as I would have regretted never having had a part of the experience. People like me can't bear to live with the "if onlys." The life of regret about our writing is more painful than taking the risks involved in going public with it.

4. *Share to enjoy its erotic nature.* It's especially appealing to some of us to read writing to a live audience because of the sensual aspect of sharing this way. Whether in print or in person, when your writings touch people emotionally and you, in turn, feel excited or satisfied by your ability to inspire their response, you're sharing for the pleasure you get from it.

5. *Share for the sake of Verity's passion.* Once, I had to decide whether or not to include one of my short stories in an anthology. I had rewritten it to the best of my ability, and I wasn't totally pleased with it. I worried it would be limp beside all the other stories and that I wasn't setting myself high enough standards for publication. But there was something I couldn't explain that urged me to include my piece in the collection anyway. When I mentioned my ambivalence to a group of writers I knew, one of them, Verity, told me this story: There was a book Verity was passionate about, a book that she held dear as one of her all-time favorites. She recommended it to everyone she knew who loved writing. All those who read the book had similar reactions—they enjoyed the author's other books enormously but found the one Verity loved flawed, weak, even mediocre in comparison. Nevertheless, Verity told me, she is so grateful that the author wrote and published the book, even if she is the only person in the world whom it touched so deeply and completely. Verity's name means truth. I decided to let

my flawed short story stay put, in case there was one person out there who needed it.

Sometimes writers share to learn whom they speak for and whom they speak to. As you notice who welcomes your work, you realize your gifts and mission as a writer. Maybe your role is to inspire middle managers to take social action in their workplace or to explain complex engineering concepts to do-it-yourself home builders, or to support appreciation of elderly people through your portrayal of them. When you discover your audience, you're connected to the community for whom you're writing. The urge to write is a call to look further than the surface of life. Writing with integrity and authenticity requires that you open yourself up, first to yourself and then to others.

6. *Share as a way to right something.* What compels many of us to start writing in the first place is that it can help to right a wrong, as in an injustice or a trauma. The injustice or trauma could be personal, such as the death of a loved one, or communal, such as racism in the justice system. Either way, your sense of doing your part in the healing process isn't fulfilled until you make your act of writing/righting public, by adding your words to the scheme of events.

When you go public, you exercise freedom by daring to expose your beliefs, values, and loves. You're not waiting for someone else to agree with you before you speak out. Your sharing encourages others to speak out, support that we need because we get a conflicting message from society that admires independence and individuality in a person but wants us all to conform to the same values. Writers wrestle with such conflicting messages, and by example, we urge other people to do the same when we make writing public.

7. *Share to evolve personally.* From this perspective, you share because either you hear your own writing differently when it's before an audience or your audience enlightens you through their comments and reactions to your writing. For example, reading a Robert Frost poem at a friend's wedding, I heard aspects of the poem I hadn't noticed even during the many times I'd practiced it before the ceremony. And through readers' responses to *Room to Write*, I learned what my next writing book would be about.

Whatever your reason to share, going public is always a risk, but a worthwhile one. You've probably taken equally useful chances in other areas of your life for the sake of business, personal growth, or love. For most of my adult writing life I've worked with young people as a visiting poet in schools. I do it because I believe that as a poet, part of my job is to help people connect to poetry early in life. Still, as I stand in front of a classroom of eighth-graders ready to excite them about writing and reading poetry, I often feel ridiculous. With my graying hair, hopelessly un-hip clothes, and constant hand motions, I'm self-conscious. The futility of my venture creeps in: How can I get thirty kids to like poems? I can't. In fact, that isn't really the point. My job is to embody the passion I hope they experience. My duty is to unabashedly expose my love of poetry to hundreds of kids every year, pour out my joy for about a week and then walk away. I plant thirty seeds per class without knowing which, if any, will ever take, and I rarely find out. It's an act of faith, of humility, of passion: It's sharing writing.

When you share writing you never know who else it will affect, but you can be sure it will affect you. I once got an e-mail from a friend who found me quoted in a handmade book she noticed in an art gallery in Texas. I'd never met the artist who made the book. But she and I are connected by her use of my words in her creation. Because she quoted me, people experience my words in a different context than their original one. I feel a sense of both delight and reverence at the way the written word acts as an emissary between strangers. Whenever we share writing we're reaching out to others without knowing whom we're going to touch or when. Sharing is our part as writers in keeping the original World Wide Web—our collective consciousness—intact.

Practice

∾ TRY WITH A LITTLE HELP
  FROM YOUR FRIENDS

Through writing, you enter a new covenant with the written word. But you aren't the first person to do so. Make a list of the writers you've fallen in love with, going as far back in your life as your memory permits. These authors all made the covenant, too, the one that includes doing their part to bring the written word into the rest of the world. They can help you recognize your part. Look over your list and ask yourself what you have in common with these writers. See if you write about a similar theme or subject matter or in the same genre or style. Have you ever read their biographies or autobiographies? Based on what you know about these authors, see if you recognize something of your own relationship or approach to writing in theirs.

When I thought about Rainer Maria Rilke, the first author on my list, it was hard for me even to consider looking for similarities between this literary master and me. At first, all I could remember was how much I loved his book *Letters to a Young Poet.* But even that was enough of a start. Those letters were written to mentor a young poet. I realized that I also fulfilled a part of my public role as a writer in a way that was related to how Rilke did it by being a writer in the schools.

Dr. Seuss, the popular childhood favorite, is an author who often appears on people's lists. He has supplied various lessons about sharing to writers who do this exercise, including not to give up on publishers. His first children's book went to seventy-nine of them before it was accepted. And then there's the novelist I know whose list of authors were all playwrights. His list taught him that he needed to write and stage plays. He started writing plays for every opportunity he could find, including his children's school productions, holiday celebrations at his place of worship, and clever training skits at his workplace. Eventually, he got a job writing scripts for films and dramatic productions at his city's historical museum. Your list of writers will guide you in a direction to begin to fulfill your public role as a writer.

private *&*
guards

∿ SHARE AND SHARE ALIKE

The very same difficulties you have with sharing in other areas of your life will affect your attitude about going public with your writing. How do you feel about sharing information? Ideas? Physical space? Your possessions? Your time? Write about your attitudes in your journal. If you are negative about sharing any of these things, is it similar to your feelings about sharing writing? In your journal, reflect on ways to separate them:

> *I hate sharing physical space. I like my belongings my way. It's true about my writing, too. I hate other people's reactions messing up my well-organized words. Rooms and writing. How are they alike? The paper and a room are roughly the same shape. That's a pretty far stretch. Oh well, why not?*
>
> *Maybe I can look metaphorically at the physical copy of the essay I'm sharing as a room that's distinct from mine. Whatever people say about the essay I could visualize as being about that particular copy. Then when I share my essay [with others], at least I can get some distance from their reactions by metaphorically giving them their own copy to mess with and keep my connection [to the essay] separate.*

When you can't separate your negative attitude from writing, try to sever the connection between the two.

> *The reason I hate sharing physical space and writing is the same. But are rooms and writing really so similar? With writing I share only when I want to, with whom I want, and for as long as I want to. Sharing the kitchen with Lisa and the kids, I don't have so much control. But sharing writing and information are a lot*

alike. And I love to share information because I really like being helpful to other people.

Once you clear your negative attitudes toward sharing your writing, you eliminate one of the major obstacles to going public.

∼ EXERCISING GOOD REASONS

More than once after hearing me present my list of reasons to share, a writer has responded, "Well, I publish to pay the rent!" I point out that nobody chooses writing over, say, being an accountant or a dental assistant as the way to pay rent. The reasons he enjoys writing, I remind him, are what nourish his ability to support himself, not his fear of an eviction notice. For some people it's painful to unearth their original reasons for sharing because they may have abandoned them long ago. Yet reclaiming your best reasons to share is a grateful reunion for your Writing Self.

We all deal with our particular pressures about being public as writers, such as fear of rejection, economic considerations, or rigid and unreasonable standards. Unchecked, they prevent you from having a stimulating relationship with your public role. To reinforce your best reasons to share writing, reread the Good Reasons list (page 158) and mark those that apply to you. Rewrite each reason on a note card in your own words and post them around your writing place. Read them every time you sit down to write until you can practically recite them from memory. You're using positive reinforcement to strengthen your connection to these reasons. It's fine if all the reasons are true for you, and it's fine if there's only one. The power of good reasons lies in your conviction about them, not in quantity.

If you aren't sure of your reasons to share, pick one from the list that you think of as admirable and try this positive reinforcement exercise, using it for a week to see if it fits for you. If not, try another until you hit on one that feels right as you repeat it to yourself. When you're aligned with a reason to share that nurtures you, the pressures that stop you from going public will ease enough to become manageable.

Sixteen

DON'T GO PUBLIC

For all the good reasons to go public, the worst reason to share is for the sake of love or recognition. Yet the hardest thing to do is to share writing without some desire for both. We all want to be loved, and we like to be admired for our efforts. It's natural. We can't help glowing a little when a publisher says yes or an audience applauds, and it's disappointing when the publisher says no thank you or no one shows up for our reading. While it isn't necessary, or perhaps even possible, to share work completely detached from the responses to it, when your desire for praise becomes a need, you have to step back from making writing public.

No matter how your writing is received, it won't satisfy your self-esteem needs. Maybe they will seem satiated in the euphoria of a great reception, but the feeling will be temporary. If you try to share your writing when your motives, consciously or unconsciously, are to feel loved and be seen, it usually has the opposite effect: You end up feeling unlovable, invisible, hopelessly misunderstood, and just a little more insecure about your writing. And if you share your writing when what you want is a pat on the back, if you don't get that pat or it isn't big enough, you end up feeling crushed. Using your writing to feel loved is like stretching a rubber band too far; the tension tears it apart.

It's true that sharing writing is an act of receiving as well as giving; when you share writing you also enrich your Writing Self. But you experience the enrichment when you're receptive to the subtle satisfactions of sharing, not when you expect it to meet desperate needs or hopeful expectations. When one of my essays appears in a magazine, I stick with how pleased I am that it found the right home. I don't allow myself to anxiously await telephone calls congratulating me on another publication. That way, if someone I know does mention that he saw the piece and what he liked about it, it's like icing on the cake instead of the whole dessert I've been dying for since breakfast yesterday.

It's easy to confuse being open to whatever recognition comes our way and being needy of it, because both states involve vulnerability. The difference between the two lies in how grounded you are in your relationship to your writing. When you try to use your Writing Self to enhance your self-image, and you make your writing public, you will always be on the lookout for someone else to respect your writing for you instead of sharing out of your own respect for the written word.

It's not just those of us who are insecure who get caught up in the love-my-writing-love-me triangle. There's enormous external pressure to attach sharing to getting love and recognition. An extreme example of how powerful society has made recognition is novelist Janet Frame's story. Having spent eight years in a mental institution, she was about to be lobotomized but was spared when her first book, *The Lagoon,* won a major literary award. We encounter variations of the same attitude about sharing legitimizing us in our own lives all the time. If someone you've just met asks you what you do and you say you're a writer, the next question is usually some version of "So, where have you been published?" The majority of the time it's not because the person is interested in reading your work. The subtext of the question "Where have you been published?" is "How impressed

with you should I be?" i.e., "How recognized are you?" This phenomenon encourages all of us to look to our Writing Self as a sanc-
tioned means of measuring our talent and worthiness as writers.

I first realized my own love triangle with sharing my writing when I
read Marge Piercy's poem "For the Young Who Want To." She says
that a real writer is the one who writes, and she calls talent an inven-
tion. Her poem ends with the lines:

> *Work is its own cure. You have to*
> *like it better than being loved.*

As I read these lines, my body still reverberates with the memory of
how much at the time I longed to be loved for my writing. It was as if
Piercy were calling me to the table, setting me the biggest challenge of
my creative life: Could I like the work of writing more than I liked
being loved? I knew that I had to stop looking for sharing writing to
supply me with the love I needed. It was a matter of separating my
longing for love from my love of writing, not of choosing one over the
other.

I often check my motives before I share by asking myself what I
want to get from making a given piece public. I know it's not the right
time if my "want" list includes items such as empathy and understanding from my audience or their appreciation and attention rather than
the opportunity to voice something I care about or to celebrate what
moves me. As you take time to become aware of your motives to go
public, you'll notice when it will be more nurturing and respectful to
your Writing Self to wait. Just as it's easier to be glad for other people's good fortune when you feel good about your own life, when you
feel satisfied, abundant, and supported as a writer, you share your
work from a state of generosity and gratitude that enriches you and
others. When you feel otherwise, sharing erodes your sense of yourself as a writer.

In order to be good for your Writing Self, sharing also has to be a mutual relationship between you and your audience. Both of you must be open to communicating. On your part, as the writer, that means being within reach of the audience's response. There's a big difference between letting your audience's reactions deject you and allowing them to influence you. If your listeners don't laugh at a comic scene, as the writer you want to be open to the possibility that the scene is not as funny as you'd thought instead of feeling mortified or jumping directly to thinking that your audience is made up of witless dullards. The interchange is blocked when you are so attached to your words that you see them as precious instead of valuable. Your sharing is lopsided because you're not open to receiving; you're open only to giving. You lose out on one whole side of the communal aspect of going public. You can't learn anything from your audience.

Another reason not to share writing is if it interferes with one of your "core values"—what matters most to you even if it's not in keeping with what society or your family or your religion promotes. A friend of mine once wrote a poem about a family member that was accepted for publication in an anthology. When she read the poem to her family and told them it would be published, they were extremely upset about it. They felt it exposed private, hurtful matters. After a great deal of thought and discussion, my friend decided not to publish the poem. But it wasn't because her family pressured her, or because she accepted the value of keeping secrets. It was because one of her core values is respecting the wishes of the people she loves, especially family, regardless of their differing views.

Writing is a fertile place to explore and challenge your and other people's values. But compromising your values in the name of creativity doesn't support either. So by all means *write* whatever you want. Go ahead and tell whatever secrets you want. It's essential to exercise that freedom. Just include contemplation time when you consider sharing what you write so that you don't end up having to choose between your Writing Self and your ethical self. The time for reflection will serve you, especially if you decide in the end that you will share your piece. You'll already feel secure in your decision if the response you get from your audience is in any way damning. When you've written something that feels very controversial and urgent, or when it's something that worries you, give yourself time to let your *true* values catch up with your desire to share. If you need help deciding what to do, you can always talk to a trusted writing partner, teacher, or counselor about it.

There's also the matter of being selective about which of your writings you share. We all write pieces we intend to make public but that never quite gel in a way we're satisfied with. All writers also create works that are for their eyes only, whether because the material is personal, raw, or for the purpose of siphoning off intense emotions or reactions to events. Psychologist Andrew Brink cites creativity as a basic human response to trauma that helps to mobilize the natural healing ability of our pysche. Author Sonia Sanchez once wrote that she probably hadn't killed anyone because she could control herself by writing. There are occasions when the only way to keep from imploding or to stay in touch with an event responsibly is to write down your reactions to it. Later, you may boycott, march, or mourn, but first you have to express, to yourself, your righteous indignation, loss, or joy. When I write for this reason, my words are monuments to the times life hasn't catapulted me into silence or into the dumbness of inertia. I don't share them with others. But I look back on these writings when I have to be reminded of my courage, when I need to be brave once again.

Finally, consider the timing for sharing your writing. Like a proud parent, you may feel a rush to show your newborn piece to the world. For you, the sheer pleasure of having finished it gives you the best energy to make it public. But you may benefit more from some private time first. When our daughter was born my husband and I didn't have visitors for the first two weeks. Our family and friends chalked up our reclusiveness to being nervous, new parents. But we needed to retreat after our child's birth for the same reason that marriage includes a honeymoon, a time for a couple to adjust to their new role as spouses. You, too, may need time to be alone with your new piece: to savor rereading it, to experience and reexperience the sensation of leafing through the pages, to glance at the completed manuscript as you go about your day, to say your silent good-byes to the characters or material you've been so intimately and privately bonded to before you are ready to offer it to others. This interval is an essential way many writers prepare their Writing Self before going public.

The main question for you to consider when deciding whether or not to share is, How will the responses of others affect me? Will I be hurt by an editor's rejection or energized by her comments? Some people won't share until they finish a piece because it disrupts the flow of their writing, while others gain momentum for their work-in-progress from getting feedback from an audience or editor. It's simply never a good idea to share your writing if you feel that the outcome will devastate your Writing Self. Even when you share your writing and it's received enthusiastically, you have to be sure not to use the wonderful reception you get as pressure to best yourself with your next piece, or that will become another obstacle as you continue to write and share.

Practice

∾ TO SHARE OR NOT TO SHARE, THAT IS THE QUESTION

It's probably impossible to be completely emotionally detached from sharing writing. But your expectations can shift from greater to lesser levels. In a way, your relationship to sharing writing is like that with someone you're close to. Sometimes you need little from each other except to enjoy one another's company. Sometimes you need more responsive attention. You can learn when not to share your writing out of neediness or in order to fulfill your expectations by identifying when you look for either in your personal relationships.

Pick one relationship from among your closest ones, such as that with a relative or a best friend. Thinking back on the relationship, write down at least ten times that you really needed the person's love and recognition, and why. Maybe there were layoffs at work, and while waiting to find out if you were next, you needed an emotional balm to ease the uncertainty and anticipation. Or maybe your loved one seemed distant and preoccupied, and you wanted his reassurance that you were still important in his life.

Write about your expectations in your journal. Knowing the patterns of your expectations in a close relationship can put you in a better position to anticipate when you might turn to sharing writing with similar expectations. Then you can decide either to postpone going public or to separate it from trying to fulfill your emotional needs.

∽ CLASHING VALUES

It is extremely important not to confuse censoring what you write with deciding whether or not to share it or with whom. That's why this next exercise is here, even though, strictly speaking, it isn't about deciding whether or not to share. You should do this exercise at this juncture if you have an overly zealous internal censor that might twist the message "Don't share without considering your values first" into "Don't write anything that might make you appear to be a bad person in your own or someone else's eyes."

Write a couple of pages that you feel are disloyal, shameful, or otherwise injurious about yourself or someone you know. You don't have to use real names. You can write in the third person: "She was so jealous of her brother that she fantasized about his death every morning at breakfast." Or you can use a fictional name: "As Elton passed by Elana, he purposely brushed the tip of his cigarette against the back of her yellow silk suit." Remind yourself that you don't have to share what you write with anyone, ever. Let yourself go. Really feel yourself rejecting any level of censorship that you encounter within yourself as a writer.

When you finish writing, make one decision: Either burn what you've written or save it in a private place. Either way, you're preventing your internal critic from censoring what you write in the name of values.

⌒ FOR YOUR EYES ONLY

The pieces you write for yourself are as important to the well-being of your Writing Self as the public ones. Some of your private writings are inspirational messages to yourself to be brave or determined or forgiving or flexible. Rereading your passionate journal entry about the injustice of a news event, your meditation on the tenacity of chickens, or your short story about an invasion of ants in your kitchen rouses an aspect of your best self. Collect these personal pieces in a file or notebook to return to and read as reminders when you need courage to write. They are proof of the power of your own written words. They are your gift to yourself as a writer. No one else ever has to read these pieces for them to make an impact.

Seventeen

YOUR AUDIENCE:
THE CONCENTRIC
CIRCLES OF SHARING

O nce you've decided that you want to go public with a piece of writing, the next question is where to share it. There are three possible audience groups that your piece could be for: one other person, your community, or the world at large. Each piece you write will speak best to one of these groups.

Imagine the three groups as the concentric circles, rippling out over a lake surrounding a skipped stone or following in the wake of a motorboat. The innermost circle is where you share one-on-one, with an audience of a single person. It is for the pieces you write in order to speak to an individual, such as the lullaby a musician may compose for his child. Letters are part of this circle. Journals and other private writings belong here, too, because the audience of one they are for is yourself. The seed of all writing begins with an urge to communicate in this inner circle in the sense that at some level we write in response to our own or someone else's need for expression. Therefore, the inner circle is the origin of *all* writing. And certain pieces you write never need to move beyond it.

The second circle, your community, is the people with whom you're already connected in some way. Your community includes family, the people in your neighborhood, and members of groups and organizations you're affiliated with. When you read a poem at a family funeral or your fiction appears in the neighborhood newspaper or your article is printed in the corporate newsletter, you're sharing in this circle. It is where you take on your public role as a writer among those you're already linked to in other ways.

The outermost circle, the world at large, is the circle of people you don't know and may never meet. These are the people who may buy your book or read your article in a magazine. They go to see your play or they see your haiku printed on a billboard. The world at large is the circle many people strive to share within. On the surface it appears to be the most glamorous, legitimate, and affirming of one's Writing Self. When people ask me how to get published, they usually mean how do they join this circle. I like how writer Nancy Aronie answers this question: Write what publishers want! But seriously, this circle is no more or less important than the others. In each circle, you do your share to keep the written word alive and well by bringing it to others.

To understand the relationship among concentric circles, think of a group dance at a celebration. From Jewish weddings to Indian ashrams, at the height of the festivities, people inevitably start dancing in circles within circles. The circles form around the person being honored or the musicians providing the music. As you dance in any one of the circles, you gain energy from the center as you give your energy to it. You must have the same spirit as the dancers have for you to flourish from sharing writing. Writers in all three circles draw from the same center of potency—the written word, the central force of language. There is also a similar give-and-take between the dancers as there is among writers in each circle as the groups spur one another on. When you share writing in any circle, you add to the momentum of the written word at the same time as you get inspiration from those sharing in the other circles. Each one feeds the others: The outer circle contains and stimulates the inner circles, and the inner circles provide energy for the outer one. The stories you tell those in your community influence how strongly they identify with the stories they read by authors in the outermost circle. At the same time, the stories you read from the outer circle weave through your consciousness, influencing the stories you write.

After you write your beloved a tribute, the next time she reads a novel that includes romance, her response to it is affected by her memory of your love letter. Or, you read a novel that inspires you. In turn, you bring a part of what moved you about the novel into the next short story you write. Maybe the part is magical realism, a circular plot structure, a great deal of textural description, or the theme of desire overcoming fate. In these ways, the circles of sharing are interdependent.

Another way to understand the link between the audiences we share our writing with is to think about each group as a body of water. There are puddles, ponds, rivers, oceans, and all the tributaries, streams, creeks, and raindrops that connect them. No matter their size, they are all water. They each serve to support life. One kind isn't better than another; it's just different. The ocean can transport us to faraway places, but we still need the rain to quench our thirst. With writing, your friend may read everything published in the ocean of the world at large that he can get his hands on about adoption, but the small stream of a few journal passages you share with him about your adoption experience is what sustains him through the process. You may not be the expert on the facts and procedures, but you are someone he knows, trusts, and can identify with.

The image of circles or of bodies of water must replace any image of your audience that's ladderlike. Your Writing Self gets depressed if you view going public as climbing a ladder. Ladders aren't indigenous to the written world. Their bottom rung will chafe at your Writing Self's relationship to sharing. Ladders rarely have rungs big enough for everyone to stand on, so you end up feeling like there's limited space for you. Those standing on the rungs above you tend to inspire awe and envy, while you can see those on the rungs below you only by looking down on them. No matter where you are on a ladder, you're in the position of comparing yourself to others. You can get so caught up in where you stand that you lose all connection to sharing in order to nourish your writing, and the opposite happens: Choosing where to make your writing public creates stress and drains you.

Instead, give up your concept of one type of audience being somehow better than another. Decide where and how to share based on the best way to reach your audience. Author and storyteller Yitzhak Buxbaum is an example of a writer who makes his work available to the full range of his audience. Several of his books are published commercially, but he also writes books that he self-publishes and sells to his storytelling audiences. He doesn't buy into the attitude that self-published writing is inferior work that publishers reject. He writes, identifies his audience, and then makes sure his work goes public through whatever means will reach his readers. The result of such willingness and flexibility takes on a life of its own: When an American rabbi had to pick a single book to explain Jewish spirituality to a unique audience of one—His Holiness, the Dalai Lama—the rabbi chose Buxbaum's *Jewish Spiritual Practices.* Buxbaum had no idea that the Dalai Lama would read his book when he wrote it, but the essence of his words was energized by everything he learned from writing and sharing his other works with a range of audiences.

Buxbaum's commitment to his public role as storyteller and writer creates a momentum and conviction that nourishes his Writing Self and, by turn, his audiences, no matter who they are. Your conviction and willingness to be public for an audience of one or one million touches your readers and animates your writing, too.

Whoever your audience is, your listeners must both support you and wound you for you to be fulfilled by sharing. Not everybody realizes it right away, but when you write, in a sense you're also agreeing to be one of the voices for others. This is no small obligation. Sharing writing is a reciprocal relationship. The presence of an audience—whether it adores you, ignores you, or abhors you—affects you. Anyone who tells you that he's not affected by how his audience receives his writing is in denial.

In a way, just having an audience—whether a friend, an editor, or a crowd of strangers—supports you in that it provides attention for your writing that, in turn, encourages you to see what you've written more broadly. I can work on a piece for months, but once I send it to my editor I see it more objectively even before she's returned it with her feedback. At the same time, your readers will wound you. I don't mean that their response to your writing will necessarily be harmful; I mean that it will pierce you, as in challenge you. It isn't always comfortable: I remember one particular New Year's Eve dinner with friends and clergy having to all but stomp my feet to get two particular guests to stop conversing long enough for me to read a poem. They weren't that interested. And yet I couldn't let that stop me. It was the clergyman's role to offer a prayer and spiritual teachings before the meal, and our host's role to supply the festive surroundings and food. As a writer, and a member of the guests' community, it was my role to commemorate the occasion by inviting reflection through the written word.

There is no guarantee you will always be welcomed with open arms when you share your writing. That's why it's important to be firmly grounded in your purpose so that you aren't discouraged from participating in society as a writer.

Practice

﹏ BEYOND GO FISH

Sometimes the way to choose your audience is by trial and error. You send your piece to various publications that reject it, but your local weekly accepts it immediately and asks for more. Or the opposite happens, and the piece you write for your weekly is picked up by one of the wire services and ends up with a worldwide audience. There's nothing wrong with the casting-your-line-to-see-who-bites method of finding your audience. To some degree, we all fish. But cultivating an audience consciousness before you choose how to go public does relieve a layer of the anxiety or frustration you can experience during your search.

Practice choosing your circle of sharing. Look at your latest finished piece. Ask yourself the following questions:

Who does it speak to? For example, if you're writing about community building, while you may feel that every community needs to do this, the audience for your writing might be specifically just those people whose community needs repair. They're the ones who are actively looking for help.

Who does it speak for? Consider your point of view. If you're a man, a Buddhist, a farmer, does the perspective you're coming from suggest an even more specific audience? Maybe your piece sheds light on the male way of building community or on the similarities between building community and permaculture farming. Answering these questions helps you focus on whom to share your piece with.

Where are these people? Make a list of all the venues that reach out to the audience you've identified. Is there a website, a print publication, an event, a radio show, a place where they gather regularly? Do you know one or more members of your audience personally?

What's the best way to reach them? Your goal isn't always going to be to reach as many people as possible. Sure, it would be revolutionary for all the neighborhood associations in your city to know about community building from a Buddhist perspective. But if you offered a lecture at the town hall, would association representatives come? It is more likely that members of the local Zen center would come to your presentation and actually apply your ideas in their neighborhoods.

Once you have an idea of the possible ways to reach your audience, you can make the choices that fit best with your particular strengths in your public role as a writer. If you love a live audience, pick a way to present your work in front of people. After going through this exercise a few times, it will become a natural part of your process of going public to be more even-keeled and deliberate in choosing the circle to share your writing in.

AUDIENCE RATINGS

When I stood to read a poem at a New Year's Eve celebration and the guests wouldn't stop talking, I was hurt and embarrassed. But I didn't let them or my feelings stop me. I took them as a challenge to meet my public role as a writer better. Maybe I didn't stand up to read with enough conviction. Or maybe the purpose of my reading that night was to remind everyone that sometimes we must rise above resistance to be heard.

Reflect back on the first and the last time you shared your writing. How did each experience support your Writing Self? How did it wound your Writing Self, or change you? Make three columns on a piece of paper and write down in the first column how each audience supported you. Perhaps one of your sharing experiences is that an editor read your story. In your first column, you would write down that the editor took time to pay attention to your work. In my New Year's experience, my support was the rest of the guests who listened attentively.

In the second column, describe how your audience wounded you. Maybe the editor rejected your piece with three specific criticisms, wounding you by pointing out what she felt were unfinished aspects of your story. For me, two people wouldn't stop talking to listen—wounding me by giving me the impression that they didn't value what I had to offer. Sometimes when I give a reading I'm wounded by the opposite experience—a person telling me my writing moved him to tears. The wound comes out of recognizing the effect of speaking out.

In the final column, write down what writing results followed your sharing experiences. For example, you rewrote your story based on the editor's suggestions and now you like it better. After my New Year's experience, I learned to look for new ways to engage my audience before I shared. As you come to expect and appreciate the three aspects of an audience's impact on you, sharing writing will get easier.

Body-Mind Exercise

∼ TEST THE WATERS

There's nothing like firsthand experience to help you become more comfortable being public and align your relationship to your audience. At a certain point you have to jump in and do it, or at least get your feet wet. A useful way to begin is to try out each circle of sharing. Try them in the spirit of doing fieldwork or research. You are gathering information to help make going public a lifelong nourishing experience for your Writing Self. If you already have sharing experience, use this exercise as a way to test out any new perspectives on sharing that you want to adopt.

Pick one person to share a piece of writing with. Be deliberate in giving it to him. Say in no uncertain terms that you want to read him the piece or that you are giving it to him to read. Pick someone you are comfortable with and who you feel will appreciate the opportunity.

Next, decide on a way to share within your community. You might read a piece to a group of friends and family during a celebration or contribute a piece to a work-related publication or one that your place of worship produces. Finally, arrange to read your writing or someone else's to people who you feel would enjoy it at a venue where you are more anonymous: a senior center, a prison, a childcare center, a hospital, a corporate cafeteria during lunch, a factory canteen during break. Keep your reading short, no more than twenty minutes.

After sharing in each circle, record how you felt about the experience. Be sure to include what you felt nourished you, what challenged/wounded you, and what you want to do the same and differently next time. Keep these notes as a reference to look back on as you go on to choose where to share and with whom. And don't forget to congratulate yourself for taking the plunge.

Eighteen

SUCCESS SHARING

Y ou will be most successful in the public arena of writing if you can expand your idea of what success means. We each have our own definition. For one person, success is publishing a book with a renowned publisher. For another person, it's getting paid to write. But even such seemingly clear goals have a tendency to get slippery as you meet them. You get a contract with a prestigious publisher, but it's for a paperback book, not a hardcover. You get a check for your magazine article, but it's not a substantial enough amount for you to feel professional. At times it seems impossible to feel successful. The balance rests in allying your mission and methods.

Missions and Methods

In order to choose circles to share in that foster your Writing Self, you must first distinguish between your mission and your methods. Your mission is your larger purpose for writing. It is your heart's concern that drives you to write. For me, it's perspective. At some level everything I write is about looking at my subject from a different angle. For someone else it might be transformation, perseverance, continuity, healing, or joy. Your mission may change of its own accord over time, but you cannot alter it by your will alone. Your mission is intrinsic to your being.

Your methods are how you fulfill your mission, including the genre you write in and which circle of sharing you pick to deliver your message. Your methods may be your own, or others may have imposed them on you, like your mother's idea that you're the next Shakespeare, or society's message that significant writing is what appears on the Sunday paper's best-seller list. Either way, your methods are choices you can change.

One of my students, Anouk, knew that her mission was to inspire people to care for the environment. Her chosen method was to publish a collection of stories about green living that gets millions of people to take new environmental actions. Although a few of her short stories were published—one on an Internet site, one in a local literary journal, and another in an anthology about trees—she couldn't find a publisher for the collection. Anouk's method was frustrating her mission. She realigned her methods. She made a list of other possibilities:

1. edit an anthology of other people's environmental stories and poems
2. write a book of meditations on caring for the environment
3. write a children's picture book
4. create a website on which to post my stories weekly, with a bulletin board for discussion
5. find a weekly newspaper to publish one story a month for a year as a guest column

Though she greatly expanded her genre methods beyond fiction, all of her venues were in the world-at-large sharing circle. Anouk thought about why. "It's a combination of wanting to reach as many people as possible and to feel legitimized as a writer," she realized. To prevent the latter from overshadowing her mission, she decided to challenge her third-circle prejudice by making a short list of one-on-one and community venues she felt would help to advance her mission. She came up with the following ideas:

1. incorporate my story about kitchen scraps into an interpretation of the Passover story to read at next year's Seder
2. read one of my stories at a local Earth Day event
3. make birthday, anniversary, etc., cards for family and friends that offer meditations on helping protect the earth

Now Anouk could explore alternative methods for fulfilling her mission, and new opportunities arose as a result. She and an artist friend collaborated on a successful line of greeting cards called Earth-Lover. Through her Earth Day reading, she was approached to lead a nature-writing workshop at a local writers' conference. Several people who visited her website reported back that they had added new earth-friendly practices to their lives.

For the remainder of this chapter, don't think of yourself as a "writer." Instead, as you consider the best ways to share your writing, see yourself as a tender of language, caring for the written word as a beekeeper tends to her hives.

Speaking on the radio program "Poets in Person," poet Sharon Olds said she'd once heard that every poet had an audience of about twenty thousand. I took this to mean that there were probably twenty thousand people who could relate to each poet's work. Olds emphasized the importance of not making a big distinction between actually connecting with these twenty thousand people and simply knowing they are out there. During the same program, she talked about her growing sense of contentment in knowing that after her death there would always be others to carry on the work of making poems.

In each of these ways, Olds's view of her contribution as a writer is as a small part of an ongoing whole. Olds is touching upon the anonymous aspect of writing: Even as we decide who we will share with and why, each of us, on some level, also has to share for the sake of language as a whole, or for the good of the idea we are writing about. Otherwise, we get caught up in our ego. The ability to act anonymously is a value in almost every set of spiritual teachings that nurtures your Writing Self as well. Just as to write is to affirm the value of language, on one level sharing affirms the importance of community. Ask yourself which is more important to you, to be acknowledged for your ideas or to communicate them to others? Would you still long to have your book published by a major publishing company without your name on it? You don't really have to decide between them to be happy sharing your work. But by gauging how much value you place on each of them, you can tell to what degree your desire to share is to bolster your personal sense of importance. Such desire gets in the way of your being fed by your sharing choices. Acknowledging your need for recognition lessens your attachment to it when you make sharing decisions.

The next step to factor in to how to share writing successfully is exploring your personal limits and strengths in going public. When I was fresh out of creative writing graduate school, a poet whose work I admired counseled me to submit my poems for publication only in the most prestigious magazines. "Why not go for the best?" he suggested. Since I was likely to get many rejections early in my career, they might as well come from the cream of the crop. That way, when a poem of mine was finally accepted, it would appear in one of the top venues. At the time, this sounded like a smart strategy. And it was a perfectly reasonable plan—for someone else. I was hurt by the number of rejections, uncomfortable with the networking involved in meeting editors, and frustrated with not having an audience for my poetry. I wanted to see one of my poems appear in *The New Yorker* as much as the next poet, but I was more eager for my poems to reach others.

Looking back, I was motivated to take my friend's advice, because I'd given up dancing professionally without ever auditioning for the companies I admired out of my insecurity about being technically good enough to dance with them. I attempted to make up for that mistake by aiming high as a poet. The problem was, I couldn't do the audition process with poetry, either. Other fine poets I know can handle it. And it turned out that I could handle it, too, when it came to proposing book ideas to publishers, essays to radio stations, and queries to magazines—just not with my poetry.

For a while, I quit submitting my poems for publication anywhere because I felt so emotionally depleted by the rejection. But that didn't feel right, either. I decided to consider stiller waters. Now I send my work to smaller publications, give readings, collaborate with musicians, and explore visual mediums for my poems. My choice hasn't made me any less of a poet or any less successful as a poet. In fact, it puts me back in touch with my mission as a writer by taking the pressure off to achieve it through a method that wasn't suited to my personal makeup. Though I could also have challenged myself and really worked at shifting my attitude, I wasn't motivated by a pressing need to push those limits with poetry.

We don't all need to win a Pulitzer Prize to be nurtured by sharing writing. There are countless alternatives that respect both our strengths and our limits. For example, what about all the people who have been writing exclusively personal journals for ten to twenty years? Their writing is a completely private experience. Maybe they participate in the community circle of sharing by reading other writers' work at the ceremonies and life passages of their family and friends. Their role in bringing the power of the written word to rituals nurtures their own commitment to their journal-keeping. It gives them a way to contribute to their community through something they love and value. After years of picking out writings for such occasions, one journal writer I know started receiving e-mails from friends of her family all over the world asking for suggestions of readings for their celebrations. She's now compiling a list of pieces for various ceremonies, and her family is encouraging her to edit an anthology.

For a long time, writer Natalie Goldberg would give poetry readings only when she could bring a friend to sit in the audience as she read, someone who would run up to Goldberg afterward, give her a big hug, and tell her she was wonderful. She respected her limit of feeling insecure reading her poems to an audience, but she didn't let it stop her. Instead, she found a way to work with it.

Artist and spiritual counselor Dana Anderson shares writing creatively in the world at large. She designs and assembles calendars by selecting twelve quotations from artists and sages and, using handmade rubber stamps, stamping a quote for each month. Though not her own words, this loving, meditative act of passing on the wise words of others is the way she honors her Writing Self's role in sharing. At the same time that she's illuminating the physical beauty of written words for others, she is also fulfilling part of her artistic calling, and the quotations that she chooses reflect perspectives that she uses to counsel others. At every level her calendars express and communicate her purpose and her mission. They also allow her to do so without having to conform to publishing policies or marketing strategies that conflict with her own values.

Beware of Ranks and Hierarchies

Don't choose sharing venues by ranking them based on your idea of their status. The world is full of pecking orders that give people power, position, and identity, so it's a challenge not to limit yourself by automatically categorizing the one-on-one, community, and world-at-large sharing circles as okay, better, best.

To move beyond confining measures of success, question your tendency to think in hierarchies. Consider the one-on-one circle and ask yourself, What if the only person I ever move with my writing is myself? Is it a failure or a waste of my time to be able to articulate in words what I feel deeply about in a way that helps me be more present in the world? What if my wife is the only person I make laugh with my stories? Won't her laughter bring lightness to my life and to others? Doesn't the way I transform grief in my poems contribute to the compassion I offer others in mourning? Through these questions you understand how sharing your writing in the inner circle has a ripple effect by association as it impacts you or one other person.

Sharing in the community circle can be more fulfilling than being public in the world at large, because the interaction with your audience is personal. While I certainly won't discourage you from pursuing what I myself pursue by way of publishing, sharing in the outer circle doesn't wholly satisfy my Writing Self or that of other writers I know because of the lack of intimacy. Despite the fact that writer, artist, and filmmaker Lisa Lewenz creates internationally acclaimed work that is seen by millions of people, she faithfully shares in the community circle through an annual April Fools' postcard she writes, designs, and sends to her friends and colleagues. No matter how tight or overwhelming her commercial deadlines, she makes time for her cards. They are her way to use her creativity to connect to her personal community and offer us all a grin.

A writing group that calls itself the Bridge Poets hosts an annual reading of the members' work exclusively for their friends and colleagues. They rent a hall, print invitations, and provide food, drink, and live music for their presentation. It's an event that people in their community look forward to. For some members of the audience it's the one time a year they experience poetry. If you think about it, being responsible for the one and only time another person relates to poetry is a meaningful role. There's no greater satisfaction from being one of the many voices in the anonymous world of outer-circle sharing.

We have a similar tendency to rank the genres of writing. One writer I know wrote acclaimed nonfiction, a novel, and prize-winning short stories. In the sense of being published, he was accomplished in several areas. But he didn't feel successful, because writing and sharing in those genres didn't invigorate his Writing Self. It caused him stress. Then he happened upon performing his writings as monologues. The first time I saw him onstage I knew he was in his element. All the strengths of his writing came through his voice, his timing, his body language, his facial expressions. He was a born storyteller, and it took him nearly twenty years of experimentation to realize it. He hadn't tried writing monologues for so long because he hadn't considered that kind of writing as legitimate a genre as literary novels or plays.

My favorite reminder to share outside of creative hierarchies is sequestered in a nearby park adjoining the local elementary school, on a bench that faces the playground. Attached to the back of the bench is a life-size bronze sculpture of a book. I visited the playground almost daily last summer and didn't see the book until my husband told me to look for it. I know many people who've frequented that park for years and have never noticed the sculpture. The artist who made it wasn't after the biggest audience. Her piece is placed where only a few people will find it; many more will miss it. The artist didn't make the piece to be seen; she made it to be discovered. So, too, not every writer needs to write, or should write, to be in the window of a mega-bookstore. The success of the bronze book depends on the artist's intention for it to stay *out* of the limelight.

One technique for getting out from under the limits of ranking is to write out what your personal sense of hierarchy looks like and then to defy it. Start by listing every writing genre you can think of and ranking them in order of importance. Most people put literary novels at the top and genre fiction farther down. Take the top three and the bottom three on your list and spend some time finding exceptions to the rule. For instance, think of a literary novel that you found unremarkable and a genre novel that is a seminal book. It's fun and even more enlightening to do this exercise with others. Everyone does the first part on his or her own, and then you all gather as a group to find as many exceptions as you can to one another's rankings. Try the same exercise ranking possible venues for sharing: books, the Internet, open readings, etc. Once you see your prejudices and dispel them, you will see options in genre and venue that never occurred to you before. One of them could be the natural fit you've longed for.

Third-Circle Publishing Realities

Many writers get so frustrated trying to join a specific realm of the world-at-large circle of going public—the major magazine and publishing houses—that I feel it's important to dispel certain myths about this arena of sharing before you can make informed choices. People often tell me stories about their bad experiences looking for agents and publishers. These writers are hurt, insulted, and angry. They feel left out. They want to know, Is my writing really that bad?

I ask them two questions. First, how many times have you picked up a novel someone recommended and put it down thinking something like, Flimsy plot, or Too much description, or Not another college-campus story, or It's okay, but I don't know what all the fuss is about? The answer is always the same: a lot of times. My second question is, When it comes to deciding what should and shouldn't be published, what's the difference between your opinions about what you read and the agent's, editor's, or publisher's? My answer is, your job descriptions. Everything else, like the trends in publishing in general and what a particular imprint is publishing, you, too, can learn from reading trade magazines and publishers' recent sales catalogues. In other words, the people who pick what major publishing companies print are people just like you, with their own particular tastes and bottom lines.

One of the countless examples of how a wonderful manuscript gets passed up is a letter to a friend of mine's agent from a senior editor at one of the big publishing houses. He called my friend's novel "lyrical and haunting" and "beautifully rendered." He went on to say how much he and several others admired the book. Nevertheless, he rejected it because he felt the novel was too understated and subtle for today's "perilous" publishing market.

On the flip side is my cousin who wrote an article for a Sunday newspaper magazine. The day after it came out she was bombarded by phone calls from editors and agents soliciting her to write a book on the subject of her article, a book she hadn't even thought of writing. One of my friends signed a contract to write a book that was then canceled because the publisher felt the subject was losing its popularity. And then there's the book proposal my agent loves. She finds an editor who adores it, too, and wants to publish it. But at the editorial board meeting the members of the marketing and accounting department won't give her the okay. Right now, a member of my writing group is looking for a publisher for her terrific manuscript about second families. The difficulty, according to more than one source, is that editors at the big publishing houses are too young to appreciate the topic.

Another reason some writers feel frustrated by publishing is that they build their expectations of success on the publicity that *sells* books. For example, the author of a best-selling memoir is touted as a former high-school English teacher, and you picture a man earnestly explaining Chaucer and grading papers for thirty years while his own story burns inside him, waiting to be told. Maybe you even imagine him, like you, writing late into the night on weekends. It's a very romantic image. He's Everyman but he's also special. If he can do it, you reason, why can't I? Maybe you can. But what you don't hear much about this author is that he's a playwright as well as an English teacher. And that he had an off-Broadway play produced before he wrote his memoir. And that he was already a member of the literary world he took by storm with his memoir. In short, this man has been writing for years!

Good publicity, like any other good writing, is selective, and since we all love a rags-to-riches tale, whenever possible the same story is told. But it is a story. The fact is that well-known writers work hard, for many years, and have failures and minor successes before they ever write a book that gets a lot of attention. Best-selling author Thomas Moore, whose book *Care of the Soul* practically put the concept of soul back into mainstream culture, had authored four books beforehand that most people have never heard of. The majority of writers start their careers with a short story published here or an article published there, and then after a long while they publish a few quiet books or get a staff job on a magazine or begin to freelance regularly for a group of publications. Every professional writer who doesn't make it to the best-seller list isn't miserable or bitter about it, either, because most of them value what they do and are nourished by the work of writing.

Personally I feel fortunate that my books are published because I truly enjoy the *process* of writing a book for publication. Not everybody does. Just as some people love doing crossword puzzles while I hate it, not everyone feels nurtured as a writer by publishing with a commercial company. Although the finished book has your name on the cover, as the writer you play a very necessary but relatively small role in the process. You supply the raw material that will be shaped into a product for sale by people you don't know, most of whom you will never meet: editor, line editors, copy editors, publicity and marketing people, the accounting department, the art department, the sales representatives, and booksellers. To say it's a collaborative process is an understatement. You have to be able to let go of what you've written to be fueled by it. You have to be more interested in how an editor's sensibilities influence your writing than you are offended by her take on your work. You must be able to revel in the close attention an editor pays to your every word, even when you have to do more work on the manuscript. You must truly believe you'll learn something from it and improve as a writer from the challenge. Then you have to stay open-minded about the cover art and have respect for how the publicity people phrase the subject matter of the book.

In short, you have to love all the attention your writing is getting even if it isn't always getting strokes, and even if the attention pokes holes in your ideas about what you've written. You have to sit out of the spotlight and cooperate with the other priorities that go into book production. Otherwise, working with commercial publishers will *not* nourish your Writing Self; it will grate on your ego or break your heart.

My Writing Self is stimulated by the collaborative aspect of commercial publishing. I discover new elements of the subject I'm writing about. I also learn a great deal about craft from my editors. It isn't always comfortable, but it's always beneficial. I've seen editorial feedback make me a better writer. I think of writing for commercial publishers as being like a potter: I give my piece to the kiln knowing full well that I don't control what comes out, and I won't know what it looks like until the firing is over and the piece has cooled. During the process of writing, a finished manuscript is a finished product, but when it comes to publishing, that same manuscript is only the clay before it's been reshaped, glazed, and fired.

The Marketplace

When you envision where to share writing, you may have a narrow understanding of what the marketplace encompasses, which limits your chances for success. Think about the original marketplace: a village square where farmers and merchants set up their stalls and the townspeople haggled, bartered, bought, and socialized. In that marketplace, poets, musicians, and storytellers would offer their work and pass the hat, or they would whet their audience's appetite for a later for-profit performance. In that same square, people spoke their minds about current issues, and sometimes a crowd gathered.

That was once the only marketplace, and it's still an essential aspect of it today. As a matter of fact, my description of the market-place could just as easily be describing the Internet, a marketplace where many writers are airing their work for avid fans and surfers to read. Like Stephen King and many other authors, you, too, can pub-lish your book on-line and sell it to readers directly. There are alter-native communities all around you where you can participate as a writer. You can perform your writing at open readings at bookstores and cafés, at festivals and fund-raising benefits. Here in Portland, Oregon, there was a day for any citizen to read a poem at designated locations, including bus stops and office building lobbies. You can publish your writing on billboards or tape it to the windows of your car or house. I publish short poems in a series called Striking Words on matchbook covers that I distribute to interested organizations. I've also printed my own pieces on address labels and pasted them to the envelopes I use for my bills and other correspondence. Recently I've seen gumball machines around town that give you a piece of gum and a page of poetry and art for twenty-five cents. It's confining to limit yourself to the traditional venues for sharing writing.

There are well over ten thousand publications in the United States alone to choose from. That's why you have to look far beyond what you see on the newsstands. Contrary to appearances, those magazines aren't the ones with the widest circulations. Industry politics deter-mines which magazines appear on the stands. The New Arrivals sec-tion in bookstores is often advertising space publishers pay the booksellers for to feature one of their titles. It isn't possible to display every new arrival, and bookstores don't carry every new book pub-lished by every publishing company either. You can see why you have to explore more than what's right in front of you. After less than an hour of research, I found an alternative publication I'd never heard of in the most conventional reference book, *Writer's Market,* for each member of my writing group: *Bartender Magazine,* 100 percent freelance written with a circulation of 147,000; *Hope Magazine,* 90 percent freelance written with a circulation of 22,000; *Murderous Intent* mystery magazine, 90 percent freelance written with a circulation of 5,000; *Cigar Lifestyles;* and *I Love Cats,* with a circulation of 100,000. There was also *Miniature Donkey Talk,* 65 percent freelance written with a circulation of 4,925, for which all of us in my writing group decided to try to write something as a challenge.

Career writers constantly redefine their marketplace. Freelance writers are always on the lookout for new venues to query. Even a rejection can turn into a new market, as it did for a writer who sent queries to an editor at one magazine who didn't buy his work but suggested him as a columnist to an editor at another magazine. The life changes you experience also expand your marketplace. When my mother, who writes restaurant reviews, became a senior citizen, she opened her eyes to a whole new array of venues through which she could share her work with older people.

Sharing Respectfully

No matter who your audience, make your public crossings respectfully. Your motivation to do this has to come from yourself, not from my prompting or from the editors and agents at every writing conference who complain about submissions that arrive dog-eared and full of typos and poor grammar, or from your disdain for the writer who slouched at the microphone and mumbled her short story in between drags of the cigarette dangling from her lips. You have to share writing as fully as you can because you value the written word. When you read a piece, stand up, wait for your audience's attention, be deliberate in your stance, and be sure you've practiced your delivery several times beforehand. When you send a written piece to someone, pack it off with the same care you'd send your children on a long trip without you. For your Writing Self, success in sharing has more to do with your intentions when you write than with the responses of others.

It's easier to share respectfully where you feel most welcome and able to be yourself: where you feel glad to be at the party, so to speak. Your urge to write is your invitation. Your willingness to share your work is your transportation. Don't join the other writers and then fret about where you stand in comparison. You're not on an airplane with first- and second-class seating. You're at a party. Everyone is listening to the same band and eating the same hors d'oeuvres. If an editor doesn't ask you to dance, for goodness sake, don't stand off to the side sighing. Go out on the dance floor by yourself, close your eyes, and start moving to the music of your words. Sure, you can always find a reason to complain about the writing life, but you can just as easily find a reason to enjoy it. The choice is yours.

The experience of the writer's life reminds me of the story of the Bal Shem Tov and the water carrier. One day the water carrier passes by the Bal Shem Tov, who greets him and asks how he's doing. "Oiy-vey," replies the water carrier. "My back is killing me. I have a corn on my foot. I spilled a bucket of water on my way to the baker and had to go get another. It made me late to the butcher, who threatened to fire me, and my wife complains we can barely make ends meet on what I bring home. What a lot I have!" "I'll say a prayer for you," says the Bal Shem Tov. The next week the water carrier passes by the holy man again. This time they laugh as they exchange a few words. The water carrier thanks him and whistles a song as he continues on his way. Having witnessed both encounters, the Bal Shem Tov's students ask their teacher what powerful prayer changed the water carrier's circumstances so dramatically. He answers, "I prayed that the water carrier accept his fate."

Your fate is to write. Part of the job description is to be one of the voices in your community in whatever genre or circle you choose, as long as you *do* choose and participate. If you do so earnestly, with conviction and respect, you may at times feel foolish or uncomfortable, but you'll be filled with the very power of language you hope to impart to others.

Don't allow sharing writing to get tangled up with your ego. Sever the relationship and rebalance the energy you put into all aspects of your Writing Self—percolation, revising, and sharing—so that you flourish from your role as a writer. Stop using sharing to measure your worth as a writer. Instead of concentrating your effort on evaluating whether you're a "good" writer or a "bad" writer, concentrate on being a fulfilled writer instead of a miserable one.

Practice

∾ MISSION: NOT IMPOSSIBLE

When you're clear about your reasons to share writing, opportunities become more apparent. Focus on your mission and watch your sharing possibilities open up. Read over a body of your past work to find your mission. You will notice it most often in the message, theme, subject, or main idea of your writings. After you read each piece, write down its subject and a few notes about what you wanted your readers to understand from it. When you're finished, look for similarities. Your mission lies in the intersections between your pieces. For example, Shakespeare's mission could be described as exploring humanity's relationship to fate. Anne Rice's mission could be described as expressing the conflicts between desire and morality. If you find it difficult to get enough distance from your work to look at it this way, solicit the impressions of other people who've read your work, such as the members of your writing group.

Another way to explore your mission is to make a list of your all-time favorite books, going as far back as childhood, and look for a common theme among them. If you discover one, it may be the same theme that drives your writing; but if not, the exercise will give you practice finding the common thread before you reread your pieces to find your own. Once you recognize it you will see sharing options with new eyes informed by your mission.

∾ METHOD ACTING

The broader your concept of how to share writing, the better your chance of being successful. Make a list of the ways you like to share writing or dream of sharing it. Then make a second list of all your current criteria for what makes it okay to call yourself a writer publicly. Is it getting published? If so, write down where you need to be published. Does it include the amount of time you devote to your writing? If so, exactly how much time would this entail? Be specific. Is an hour a week sufficient? Is getting paid for your writing one of your criteria? How much would you need to be paid? Is it the genre you write in? Which genre means "being a writer" to you? What about what others think of your writing? Who has to appreciate your work for you to think of yourself as a writer?

Look over your second list and circle all the answers that surprise you. They are the hidden agendas that influence the scope of your sharing methods. Cross out any genre or venue on your list that you recognize as one that someone else has imposed on you. My grandfather used to tell my mother that she would write the great American novel and support him in his old age. It was his way of complimenting her writing, but for whatever reason, the idea of publishing a novel became a method of sharing that paralyzed my mother for years. She couldn't think of herself as a writer unless she wrote a novel. She didn't dare try a novel because of the pressure of thinking it had to be a seminal one. She was close to forty when she finally started to write and publish, and to this day she hasn't attempted a novel. Does your idea of what you must accomplish in order to say you're a writer publicly support or confine your ability to share?

Look over both your lists to make sure that your sharing methods are balanced. All your methods shouldn't be part of the world-at-large circle. Add at least one or two methods from another circle. If your list includes writing the great American novel, consider revising your goal to something like eventually writing a novel that so personally bests your past work that you deserve your own private American Book Award for writing it.

∾ LIMITS AND STRENGTHS ROAD MAP

In deciding where and how to share your writing, one of the steps is to understand your own personal limits and strengths in terms of going public. Make a list of what you see as your sharing limits and another of your strengths. Your lists can be long or short, but they must each include at least one item. Examples include:

Limits: I hate blind submissions/contests/reading aloud
Strengths: I'm good at collaborating/writing query letters/making writing into visual art

For now, put aside any sharing methods that conflict with your limits, or be creative with your method so that it doesn't compromise them. If, for example, you want to participate in a reading and you enjoy collaborating but hate to read aloud, you might ask an actor friend to read your work for you. Or, because you are brave in making your writing visual, then you can show your writing visually when it's your turn to read.

Using your two lists, make a third list of sharing methods that interest you and that also respect your strengths and limits. Pick two methods from your list to try.

∾ THE SILENCED TREATMENT

If you've been silenced by a negative experience with sharing your writing, then before you share again, devise a plan for how to take care of your Writing Self if you end up being received in an unwelcoming manner. First, journal about the piece you want to share and with whom. What do *you* want from the sharing experience? What do you think your audience wants? Beatification? Celebration? Healing? A dismantling of barriers? Help to live their lives? Are your wants and theirs at odds? Can you harmonize them in some way? Don't worry if you can't. The point of this practice isn't to appease your audience. The point is to prepare yourself to share and be nourished by it no matter how your audience behaves. After all, sometimes people react defensively when they hear a truth that they don't want to deal with; they blame the messenger.

Once you've laid out your sharing circumstances, spend some time imagining the worst-case scenario: you get booed, an editor suggests you give up writing. I don't believe that you create the future by rehearsing negative outcomes when you do it in order to prepare for their possibility. But you have to take the next step; supply yourself with a soothing perspective to draw on if the worst happens. It really works.

For a time, I was sending my poems to magazines and getting back rejection letters that said how close my poems came to being accepted. It was awful for me. I saw my poems as destined to be almost but not quite good enough. When I admitted to a fellow poet that my poems were just missing the mark every time, her perspective was that my poems had some edgy, compelling element in them that caught editors' eyes. She suggested that my poems might have something fresh to offer that needed only a bit more work on my part and more opportunities for editors to read before they felt ready to publish them. Her way of looking at the same situation put a whole new and encouraging light on it. Whose take was more accurate, my friend's or my own? It doesn't matter. Her interpretation kept me going.

We all need stories to tell ourselves so we can move on. As poet Muriel Rukeyser said, "The world is made up of stories, not atoms."

∾ SHAPING YOUR MARKETPLACE

A parent at my neighborhood elementary school asked me to participate in an event she was organizing called Guerrilla Poetry Week. All the classes made surprise displays of poetry for one another, such as hiding haikus in one another's coat pockets or on the backs of one another's chairs; pasting poems on a stairway, so that every line was on a different step, or on the windows of the school bus; interrupting another class to perform a poem; or leaving the start of a poem pasted on the back of a bathroom-stall door with a pencil for adding the next line. This parent called the right person when she called me: I have a dream of the written word being woven into our daily adult lives in a similar fashion. But I can't realize my dream alone. I need the help of every writer I can get.

Whether you want to join my cause or free up your limiting view of the marketplace, try this exercise: Write down every crazy, wild, unimaginable way you can think of to share writing publicly: sky-writing, bullhorn, an LED billboard downtown, during commercial breaks on television, printed on napkins or on flags during a parade. Work on your list for four days, adding to it as new ideas come to you. While you're at it, get a writing friend to join you by making his own list. Look at your lists together. Many of the venues will be outrageous and impossible, but a few of them will have real potential. Even an outrageous one may hold the seed of a great way to go public. Reading a short story to customers on a grocery store checkout line is an idea that could develop into getting hired to do storytelling to crowds on line for special events such as concerts or the circus. The point of this practice is to break out of conventional thinking.

Another technique for expanding your marketplace options is to work with a partner, with each of you writing down all the subjects your own writing includes: camping, cars, green energy alternatives, Japanese culture, tall ships, basketball. Then, one subject at a time, together make a list of all the venues you both can think of. For example, camping might include specialty magazines, tourism publications, camping websites, senior citizen publications ("Camping Over 50"), Pacific Northwest publications, National Parks publications, children's publications, food publications ("Gourmet Meals on a Camp Stove"), Health and Fitness publications ("Preparing to Carry a Fifty-Pound Backpack for Two Weeks Uphill"). Between you and your partner, you will probably come up with more possible venues than there are stalls at your local farmer's market!

RESPECT REVISITED

One of the hats I've worn as a writer is editorial assistant for a literary journal. My job was to read unsolicited manuscripts of poetry and fiction from people like you and me. I would pick up a big brown box full of unopened submissions from the magazine's office, and the editors would hand me an 11x14 manila envelope to mail back two weeks later with anything I thought they should consider for publication.

I was surprised at how the condition of some of the manuscripts affected my impressions of the writing. It was harder for me to focus on the writing when a strikingly poor presentation was distracting me. I had only a short amount of time to give to each submission. I found myself reading no more than the first and last paragraphs or stanzas of a manuscript if there was no cover letter, if it had typos, or if its worn condition showed it had made the rounds to many journals before it came to me. I saw for the first time that presentation and content are inextricably linked.

Think of one thing you can do to add to the way you show respect to writing when you share it. Remember to look into the eyes of your audience periodically as you read. Print your manuscript on quality paper, using a typeface and font size that are easy on the eye. Have somebody double-check your grammar, spelling, and punctuation. If you're sharing someone else's writing, present it attractively and in a way that invites listeners to explore the writer's work on their own. In all aspects, be an ambassador for the written word whenever you are in a public role.

Nineteen

SHARING
OBSTACLES

When your fate is to write, it comes with responsibilities. Responsibility to your writing can include being precise, emotionally honest, or grammatically correct. But when it comes to sharing, it's spelled "response-ability," and it means your ability to respond, as in to reply, to reciprocate, and to participate. Sharing writing isn't your reward for the efforts of writing. It is your response or your reply to the forces that persuade you to write. Sharing is the fulfillment of your partnership with the creativity that taps into you as you tap into it through the written word. You receive many gifts of insight and understanding from this relationship at the same time as being a conduit for passing on gifts. If you ignore or neglect your response-ability, you silence a part of your Writing Self by severing one of the main purposes of your falling in love with writing: to engage with others.

The catch to going public is that if it's hard for you to do, you can't just grit your teeth and do it anyway to receive the benefits. You don't grow as a writer by sharing simply by showing up to do it no matter how it makes you feel. There are conditions that block the process:

1. you're too worried about what others will think of your writing
2. praise paralyzes you
3. you feel bitter or despairing about past experiences
4. you have opposing goals for your work

Getting Past "What Will They Think?"

If you find yourself blocked by the what-will-they-think obstacle, then every time you share your writing with anyone, or imagine doing it, it feels to you like having to prove your worth as a writer—a test you're doomed to fail. We all get a little nervous about sharing writing and hope that the audience appreciates our piece. If they don't, it's natural to be disappointed. But when you've turned your writing into the proof of your worth, you feel devastated. Even more destructive to your Writing Self than how others respond to it is your own anticipation of rejection, which usually masks a fear of not being good enough—not just as a writer, but as a thinking, feeling person.

In most areas of our lives, we put a lot of value on consensus: If enough people agree with us, we gain confidence in our ideas, and if not enough people agree with us, we're more likely to question ourselves. It would stand to reason that if you could find enough people who liked your writing, you would feel confident sharing it. But such logic doesn't necessarily follow when you suffer from this obstacle to going public.

I once got stuck in the what-will-they-think obstacle before I'd even finished writing a piece. A magazine had asked me to write a millennium poem, and even though it's difficult for me to write poems for occasions on demand, I wanted to do it because as a writer I felt it was important for me to focus on this juncture of time. Trying to write the poem became more and more excruciating as the deadline got closer. Everything I wrote sounded corny. I found myself imagining the critical and dismissive letters to the editor that the magazine's subscribers would write after reading my poem. When I started fantasizing about an awkward call from my editor saying that she had decided not to use the poem after all, I realized I was so caught up in how people would judge my poem that I wasn't paying enough attention to expressing my ideas in powerful language. I also knew I was out of alignment with my Writing Self because not once did I imagine someone reading the poem and liking it.

Somewhere along the way I'd given over my creative energy to creating fear. I was afraid I hadn't anything to say about the turn of the era. I turned that alarm into the dread of my lack being discovered by others. The truth was that however my poem turned out, people would read it and some would be moved and some wouldn't—*just like every other piece of writing I or anyone else has ever written.* Once I came back to this universal writing truth, I was able to refocus on writing the poem. Until then I was busy generating all the reasons I should back out of the assignment so that I could reject my readers before they had the chance to reject me!

That's what happens when you are in the midst of this obstacle. You use your worry as a defense against the rejection that you anticipate from others. But it's actually your rejection of yourself that you're trying to stave off, and in the process you block the energizing part of being public from reaching you as well.

Other trains of thought that are warning signals that you're building up barriers include: the piece is too complex or controversial or trivial to share, what if it stinks, and what if I offend someone. Your worries can separate you from the good that sharing does for your Writing Self. To subdue these concerns, post a sign on your writing desk that reminds you of the universal writing truth: When it comes to your audience, some will be moved and some won't. What you write affects you more than anybody else.

Poison Praise

Sometimes the very attention we long for can hurt us. As author Ariel Gore points out, "Praise is kinder than criticism, but it's judgment all the same." I've had this experience in yoga class as well as with sharing writing. Week after week, I learn from the guidance and reminders my instructor offers the whole class. Nevertheless I always hope she'll give me some individual feedback. Then the moment I get my wish and she compliments me, I turn spastic; my attention to my breathing and body dissolves because I focus on her words instead. I stop doing yoga the instant the teacher becomes more important than my practice.

A related experience I have is when I tell someone I meet that I'm a writer, and he reacts with awe. Some people have a romanticized idea of me sitting at my desk in a creative trance as fully realized thoughts and sentences flow. They don't believe that what I really do is hunch over my computer screen and try to untangle my ideas and sentences in between the hours I spend on-line doing research or on the phone interviewing people. This highly complimentary vision of me does more toward making me feel like an unwilling con artist than appreciated as a writer. Now, I'm not suggesting that you avoid praise for your writing or that praise is always a destructive thing. What I want to point out is that you have to make sure you have a reasonable relationship with praise so it doesn't bite you in the backside while you're taking your bows.

For some people, praise amounts to pressure. When my friend Alan sent an editor a short story and she wrote back that the subject wasn't for her but that she loved his writing and would like to see the next story he writes, instead of feeling encouraged and excited, he couldn't finish the story he was working on. Suddenly he felt like it had to be as good as or better than the piece he'd already sent her. Alan couldn't work on his next story without comparing it to what he'd previously written. Instead of growing as a writer from the editor's compliment and interest, he was freezing up from what he saw as her expectations of his next story. In reality the expectations were his own. "I was on the line to make the story good enough for her to buy it. Her rejection would be proof that I couldn't handle writing. To disappoint an editor who liked my work was shooting my own foot. So the only way I could finish the story was to forget about sending it to her. That's when I realized I had to get a grip on how to deal with professionals liking my writing."

Praise can also be to writers the equivalent of refined sugar— totally addicting while providing no real nourishment. The attention you get from sharing your work is exhilarating. When you are listened to closely and you witness your audience respond to your words, do you feel like you're finally being seen and understood by others? Do you feel legitimized in a new way? You may discover particular elements of your writing style or presentation that intensify your audience's response, such as a staccato dialogue between your characters or making facial expressions as you read. It's good to know and utilize the elements that move your audience when you share, as long as you're doing it for them, not in order to reproduce the high you get from their reactions.

The more you use sharing to get attention, the more likely it is that you will begin to write and be public for the sake of praise. As you lose touch with all the other things you can gain from sharing, such as a connection to community and fulfilling your mission, your audience's responses will become less and less satisfying because approval alone isn't truly nourishing for writers. And, if you are focused only on praise and then you stop getting it, it can stop you from writing. My friend Ella won a prize the first time she sent an essay to a contest. She was so thrilled that she entered twelve more competitions over the next two years. She didn't win any of them: "I started to think of the initial honor as a fluke. What had been so encouraging became embarrassing. I decided those first judges made a mistake. If my writing was really prize-worthy, why hadn't I gotten so much as an honorable mention in just one of the other contests? For a long time afterward it was hard for me to trust anyone's good opinion of my writing or to make it public."

I take praise as I take honey in my tea. It's another flavor that adds sweetness to something that already warms me.

Overcoming Bitterness and Despair

In the process of looking for places to share, it's inevitable to go through a series of disappointments. When you've stockpiled them, they block you from the benefits of being public. It's hard to take in what nourishment an audience provides when it's filtered through painful memories of sharing or trying to share that still make you feel angry. If you think the bad breaks, near misses, and insensitive remarks you've endured are greater in number or magnitude than those of most other writers, then join the club! You have been hurt, you have been that close more times than you care to count, you have been ignored, you have been singled out and cut down monstrously and unfairly. So have I. So has almost any writer you admire.

If you still doubt this, attend a writers' conference. Its condensed nature creates an intense energy: all the talks to choose from, all the people to meet and connect with. Perhaps because of the sheer abundance at these events, there's a tendency for people to let loose extreme feelings. Listening to people trading stories about lousy agents, snooty editors, the real reason so-and-so got published, the real reason they themselves didn't get published (lousy agents, snooty editors, etc.) can be an enlightening and cathartic experience. You get a chance to see that you really aren't the only one who gets rejections. You meet other people who are on the fourth or fifth rewrite of their novels. You come to realize that many of your good and bad experiences in looking for ways to go public are common to most writers. On the other hand, such conversations can feed on themselves, creating an atmosphere of bitterness and despair that leaves groups of writers nodding their heads at the unfairness of it all and using unjustness as an excuse to remain bitter and sad.

The real despair doesn't come from what anyone else says or does and doesn't do regarding your writing. It comes from your own over-grown desire for approval. I was able to move through my own bitter-ness and despair only as I became less prone to feeling humiliated at the first sign of rejection and filled with grandiose fantasies of success at the smallest hint of potential acceptance. Not surprisingly, I felt more complete and satisfied as a writer as I untangled my self-esteem from sharing my writing. Then, as an added benefit, I became more successful. That doesn't mean that these days I'm immune to hurt, disappointment, insecurity, or anger. It means that I generally recover from these emotions faster and that I've learned how to put what I call "impact absorbers" between my weak points and myself when I go public.

Impact absorbers are the boundaries I create to protect myself from getting ego-involved when I make writing public. For example, I don't send my poetry manuscripts to contests anymore because I can't get past my resentment over the reading fees. Another of my impact absorbers is that my agent is under instructions not to discuss with me the details of who's interested in my book proposals. I only want to know who's made a firm offer. I've learned from experience that a publisher's interest can be subverted for a myriad of reasons. My hopes take up too much energy unless I ignore the possibilities that feed them. I take care of my Writing Self by staying as far away as I can from the almosts and if onlys, though I know many other writers who aren't bothered by them.

Getting rid of your old collection of hurts and disappointments is just as important as keeping your new reasons for feeling bitter or despairing from piling up. I found help with dispelling old demons of bitterness and despair through a combination of reading books about creativity and releasing some of my pent-up feelings of rejection in a support group. Other writers I know have written down all the situations they felt resentful about, shared their inventory with another writer, and buried or burned the list. Once you're ready, you, too, will find your own ways to stop these demons from eating away at your relationship to sharing writing.

Opposing Goals

Your Writing Self can sometimes freeze when it gets opposite signals about your goals for writing. If you're telling yourself to start writing but get it right the first time, or to go public but don't be nervous, or to be honest but don't upset anyone, make yourself vulnerable, take a stand on a value or belief, or draw attention to yourself, then you are sending your brain contradictory signals that frustrate both goals.

During a discussion about craft, one writer at the table said, If you don't aim for perfection, why bother? Her rhetorical question epitomizes having two opposing agendas for your Writing Self: Write, but make it perfect. Writing or going public while being invested in perfection undermines creativity. We write to capture a part of the chaos of life in language, not to demonstrate perfection. But if you have an idea in your mind that you can only share what you've written perfectly, you have to change it with counter-reasoning so you can write and share without an obligation to perfection.

Whatever your opposing goal, you can use alternative logic to dispel it. If your opposing goal is perfection, you might be able to shift out of it using one of these lines of reasoning:

1. Tell yourself that you're not compelled to write by the desire to meet some standard but by the need to express something.
2. Tell yourself that aiming for perfection can make you impossibly self-critical and can sabotage your ability to write and share.

3. Tell yourself that there's no such thing as perfect. It is an idea. To pretend that perfection is achievable wreaks havoc on your creativity.

However you work yourself out of it, you have to ferret out the conflicting goal you're trying to fulfill while being public. For instance, your essay is due to the editor on Friday. It's Tuesday and you still haven't written a word. You know what you want to say, but you can't get yourself to sit down and write it. Ask yourself if you've created a situation with two opposing goals. Have you turned your deadline into writing an essay that's better than anything you've ever written and proves to the editor and the rest of the world that you are a brilliant writer—and to do it by Friday? No one can meet that deadline.

Practice

∾ FIRST FACE YOURSELF

If you're like most people, you'll find that your opinions about yourself are far more important to you than are others' opinions of you. That's good news when it comes to sharing writing, because you have a lot more control over how you see yourself than you do over how others see you. When you sort out negative ideas you have about yourself from your concerns about what others think of you, you can face both types of worries and manage them.

When your obstacle to being public as a writer centers on your concern over what others will think, write down each of your "what ifs" and then write what you honestly fear the outcome of these worries will be:

1. What if I read my story at an open reading and I get booed? *It proves that I'm a lousy writer and that I shouldn't ever try again.*

2. What if I send a query letter to ten editors and not one is interested? *It means that my ideas are stale and unappealing.*

3. What if I finally get an agent and she can't sell my novel? *It means I'll never break into trade publishing.*

Once you've exhausted all your terrors, pretend they're someone else's to get some emotional distance from them. In writing, try to help this fictional other person put the what-if scenarios in a more positive perspective. For instance, if an agent can't sell your novel, it may also mean that you must now rewrite the novel one more time, or take what you learned from writing it and apply it to your next novel, or find a new agent. As you work through each item on your list, you'll be relieved to discover that none of them is as horrible or one-sided as you feared.

Now, do a variation on this exercise that explores your worries and negative ideas about yourself. First, write down how you'd like to be known as a writer. For example: "I'd like to be known as a writer who helps people be brave." Next, write down what you think is the worst thing about you as a writer. For example: "My difficulty is with two of the most important elements of writing: grammar and imagery." Finally, write down what you think is admirable about you as a writer: "I stick with it no matter how insecure or stuck I feel." Your lists may be longer than these examples.

Read over what you've written. These phrases express your wishes, weaknesses, and strengths. Acknowledging them and accepting them prepares you for going public with your writing in a grounded way. When you admit your weaknesses, you are being realistic about yourself, and you can work on improving weak areas and feeling less embarrassed about having them. You understand that all writers have flaws that they work on and that these particular flaws are yours.

Your strengths become your vehicle for realizing your wishes. When your Writing Self is aligned and harmonized, you share writing from a foundation that isn't so easily upturned by other people's opinions or your own worries.

⌁ SHARERS ANONYMOUS

This practice does double duty: It helps to antidote poison praise and it also offers a way to get over worrying about what others will think when you share writing. The goal is to share your writing completely anonymously.

You can be anonymous in several ways. For example, leave copies of one of your pieces of writing on seats in the bus, train, Laundromat, or a waiting room. Slip it inside a copy of a best-selling book at the library. Write out a poem in chalk on the sidewalk before dawn.

Over the period when you are sharing anonymously, take two five-minute breaks each day to list any insights you have about your relationship to praise or what you imagine people think of your writing as it is out there in the world unsigned. Do you feel nervous? Giddy? Angry? Relieved? Are you fantasizing about who is reading it and what they are thinking? Do you miss the praise? There are no right or wrong responses. You are simply noticing how the absence of your name or identity affects your relationship to sharing.

If you can't stand it, think of yourself as detoxing from an addiction to praise. If you feel liberated, then maybe you're getting your first taste of worry-free sharing. It's more likely that you'll have a mix of reactions. By writing them down, you can refer back to them when you start sharing using your name again. This will help you stay mindful of how praise or worry influences your relationship to sharing.

Knowledge is power. With it, you can reshape your relationship to sharing, worry and praise.

⌁ BITTERNESS AND DESPAIR

Here is a three-step process for cleansing yourself of bitterness and despair. First, to rid yourself of your stockpile of bad sharing experiences that still bother you, briefly write down each one. If you start to do this and it is incredibly painful, help yourself lighten up enough to finish: Scribble cartoon caricatures beside each incident. Find faces and images in old magazines to cut out and paste next to each item that symbolize an aspect of the incident. Or title each one with a line from a popular song or a book title: You might give the title "Ain't Misbehavin'" to the time an editor made a pass at you when you asked him to read your script.

Next, write briefly about the encouraging things that you've experienced sharing your writing. No incident is too small. Almost every time I work as a writer in an elementary classroom, the teacher sends me an envelope containing a thank-you letter from each student. I know the letters are assigned by the teacher for letter-writing practice, but there is always at least one really heartfelt letter of gratitude among the group. I count them among my encouraging sharing experiences.

When you've completed both inventories, read them to a trusted creative friend or have your friend read them to you. There is something transforming about hearing your pain and your encouragement outside the confines of your mind. Afterward, take the list of miserable sharing experiences and get rid of it: bury it, burn it, recycle it, or shred it.

Now that you've rid yourself of the painful past, the second part of this process is to read a few honest and witty memoirs of writers who talk about sharing writing, such as Anne Lamott's *Bird by Bird,* Nancy Aronie's *Writing from the Heart,* and Suzanne Lipsett's *Surviving a Writer's Life.* There is strength in numbers. Having the experiences of other writers to refer to will help cool any lingering negativity of your own that could boil up and fill you with bile and hopelessness again.

Finally, take preventative measures against future bitterness and despair. Develop a personal set of boundaries and impact absorbers for sharing your work: You won't participate in contests, for example. You will do open readings only at two specific venues, submit manuscripts only to places where you or someone you know has a contact;

you will only search for a literary agent who works outside the New York publishing world. Try not to be concerned with the consequences of setting limits. You have to listen to yourself, trust your way of operating in the world. If what you're doing doesn't work, you can always amend it. Every writer I know has their own unique story about how they sold their first book. And their stories often reflect their lifestyle.

When I was ready to write *Room to Write*, I read a how-to-get-published book that recommended sending book proposals to agents who represented similar books. It's a good idea. But at the time, this approach felt too impersonal. It didn't make intuitive sense to me. It wasn't my style. So instead, I explained my project to the few writers I knew who had agents or editors and asked them for their editors' and agents' names. I sent query letters to publishers and agents to whom I could use my friends' names by way of introduction. This approach felt truer to my experience of life—one big, connected web. My publisher and my agent came out of those letters. By coincidence, it turned out that the agency my agent worked with was run by the brother of a girl I knew from grade school, proving that my life indeed is a connected web.

If you want to avoid bitterness and despair, you have to be proactive about it. It takes work and courage to weed out the past and set limits in the present. But it's well worth the effort to get out from under a morass of negativity that infects your Writing Self and withholds from you the significance of your public role as a writer.

Twenty

FINAL WORDS

Leading a long and productive writing life has less to do with the amount of talent you have and everything to do with your staying power. A dear friend tells the story of a college class-mate who was clearly the least talented member of their drama department. This woman got the smallest roles in all the productions, and she was given more than her share of stagehand duties. But she also worked harder than anyone else on her lines and acting exercises, and most of the time she did it with enthusiasm because she loved theater and acting.

Ten years later, my friend tells me, this "untalented" actress acts for a living. She still doesn't get leading roles, but her acting improves all the time, and she is doing what she loves. Not one of the other members of her class—including the star students with much-lauded natural talent—became professional, working actors. It was this student's dedication and passion for acting that propelled her to fulfill her dream. It was her tenacity mixed with her reverent connection to how her art form affects her. All the talent in the world is useless without developing these qualities. So are all the lucky breaks.

Whether you do it professionally or for your own pleasure, writing is no different. If you love it, then love it. The parts of the writing process that confound you will eventually nourish you, if you approach them as your teacher instead of as your problem. As Marge Piercy says in her poem "The Art of Blessing the Day," "What we want to change we curse and then pick up a tool. . . . If you can't bless it, get ready to make it new." You're ready now. You have the tools. I wish you well.

... the morning pages and the various journals I've written to silence that critic's rising my critic who writes and the critic's hard on me. This critic has sabotaged my brain; I can't think. Words come slowly or not at all. Writing becomes a burden — I am a screenplay. Logic elude me too. How can I shape the critic's them loose. We choked my voice

About the Author

Bonni Goldberg is the author of the best-selling books, *Room to Write, Gifts from the Heart,* and *The Spirit of Pregnancy.* Her essays, fiction, and poetry have appeared in newspapers and magazines and on public radio. She's been awarded numerous prizes for her own writing and teaching as well as for innovative programs presenting the written word in unconventional formats and locations. She has been teaching writing for more than fifteen years. Ms. Goldberg lives in Portland, Oregon, with her husband, artist, writer, and sometimes collaborator, Geo Kendall, and their daughter.

Re-vision when trying so to see again. I know my arguing ideas are pretty bare-bones and documented — as if music in a video of more by Numerals.

So, once an idea emerges with some stability to it, some sense of a permanent grounding to something in my mind, electric current I watch the idea down. If I'm really doing it, like magnetizes other ideas of it, the or what. Perhaps all of no clue I get really this chance in one sitting after that comes a kind of writing combat zone. Has the idea/idea/idea made any magic to them, or staying power. Can I re-capture the original thought that began this "poem" had it moment as it turned by if. True, there are ever and a first slight appear, find myself in that short corperies line, myself in writing, the re-visions. Aspect of writing.